American Prisoner of War Camps

in Idaho and Utah

Kathy Kirkpatrick

America Through Time®
Adding Color to American History

For Jinger

America Through Time is an imprint of Fonthill Media LLC
www.through-time.com
office@through-time.com

Published by Arcadia Publishing by arrangement with Fonthill Media LLC
For all general information, please contact Arcadia Publishing:

Telephone: 843-853-2070
Fax: 843-853-0044
E-mail: sales@arcadiapublishing.com
For customer service and orders:
Toll-Free 1-888-313-2665

www.arcadiapublishing.com

First published 2018

ISBN 978-1-63499-041-7

Typeset in Minion Pro 10pt on 13pt
Printed and bound in England

Contents

List of Illustrations

Introduction

America is a nation of immigrants, so hosting prisoners of war (POWs) from their homelands brought mixed feelings among the civilians and military in the communities where the prisoners were housed and worked. For many Midwestern farmers, being able to contract for German POW labor not only eased the labor shortage, but it also brought the opportunity to speak their native language, perhaps to learn about family and friends left behind when they immigrated to America. It also often gave them the opportunity to provide additional food for men who worked hard for them and shared their friendship. Although these Americans had sons fighting in the war, they were more aware of the lack of choices these German prisoners had in their own lives than those who had not left an oppressive homeland.

The same situation applied to Italian immigrants and Italian POWs with the additional benefits of a less strained relationship after Italy became a part of the Allied cause in September 1943. The resulting friendships (and some marriages) show the very positive results of their experiences under very difficult circumstances.

In fact, when German-American or Italian-American families were given permission to hire prisoners of war to work on their farms or canneries, they were being given a measure of approval often missing in their own communities. 330, 000 Germans had registered as aliens in 1940, and 694,000 Italians. Those not living on the coasts were not displaced, but suffered the name-calling and ostracism promoted by the government and media directed at those groups of people during that time to promote the war effort. They could be arrested just for translating English into German for an aged grandparent.

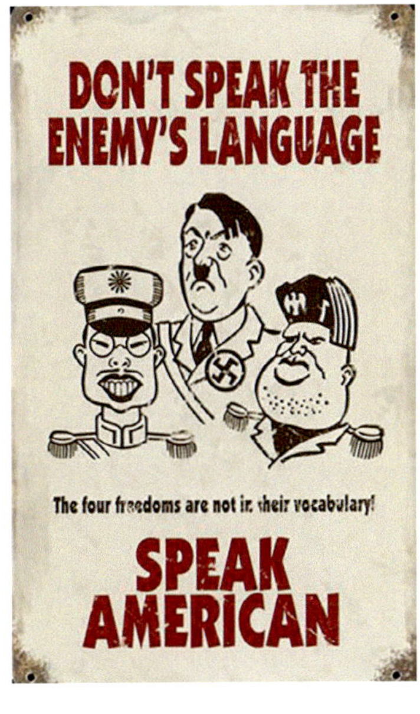

From "Una Storia Segreta" by Lawrence Distasi. The licensing metadata from the picture claims that it is a "work prepared by an officer or employee of the United States Government as part of that person's official duties."

The stories shared in the course of researching this topic include a moving description by a young Girl Scout raising the flag while a truck load of prisoners passes by, with tears in their eyes. Even as a child, she understood that those men deeply loved and missed their children now living in harm's way.

Following the war, some of these farm families corresponded with the former prisoners until their deaths. A treasure trove of about 350 letters and photos from German former prisoners has recently been discovered in a home in Tennessee. They are now housed at the Lipscomb University in Nashville. They'd met by working on that farm, and kept in touch over the years. But it was secret. The letters were found in a cereal box in a closet and even the children of this woman didn't know about them.

For many years into the 1970s and 1980s, as late as 2009, there were reunions and family trips made by former prisoners to their old camps and the farms where they worked. They also visited the graves of their comrades who didn't survive to go home at the end of the war.

Also, of the half million Germans immigrants arriving in the United states from 1947-1960, several thousand had spent time here as prisoners of war. The same can be said of Italian immigrants after World War II. They had friends and good experiences here that motivated them to move here themselves.

Even among those enemy aliens who were forced to "repatriate" at the end of World War II in exchange for Americans and for other reasons, the vast majority had agreed to the arrangement because it guaranteed them the ability to return to the U.S. at a later date. They later used that agreement to return home to the United States. That included Germans, Italians, and Japanese.

Prisoners were moved between Service Command Areas in 1943 as we built more camps and received more prisoners from overseas. Later, the prisoners were moved within a Service Command as necessary to provide seasonal labor on farms and in canneries as well as other work necessary for civilians as well as the military population.

Using a variety of sources in the United States and Italy, the complete story will be told. Sources cited include military records now housed at the National Archives II (College Park, MD), documents from the Italian Army Archives in Rome (*Stato Maggiore Esercito*), *L'Ufficio Informazione Vaticano per I prigionieri di guerra istituito da Pio XII* in the Vatican Secret Archives, books, articles, websites, and photographs.

Also utilized are interviews with former POWs, guards, translators (and their families) and many other sources both published and unpublished. Their experiences will also be compared to those of German POWs and internees held in America during World War I.

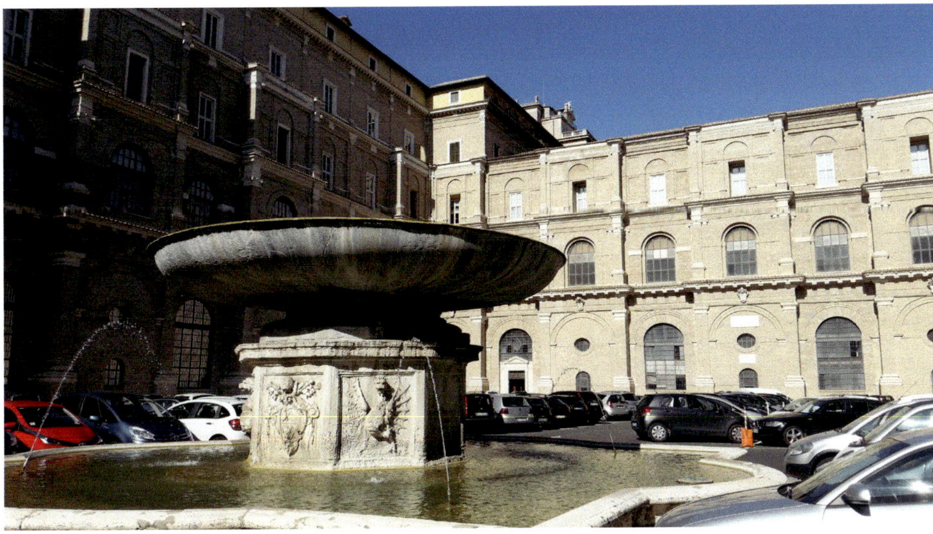

Entrance to the Vatican Secret Archives, photo by author.

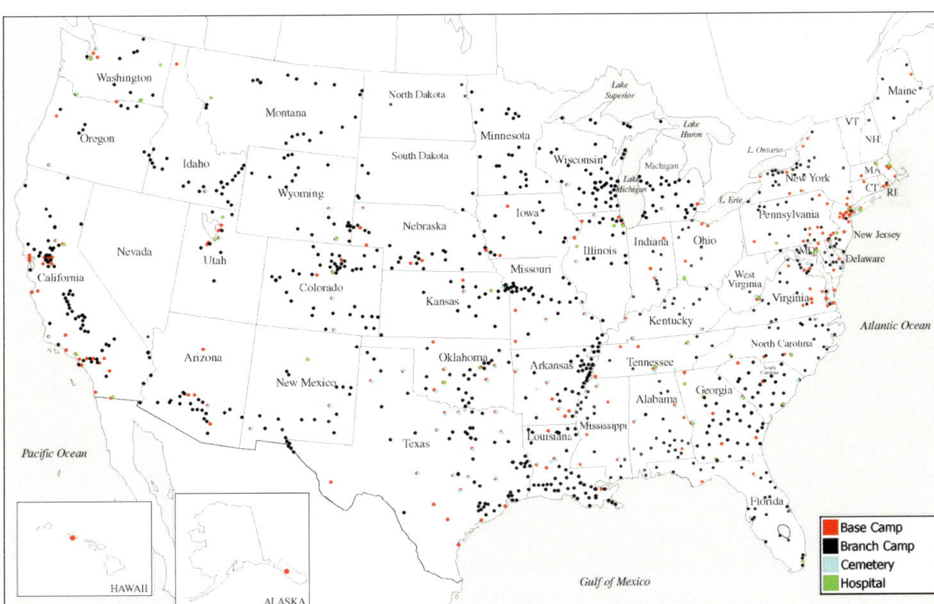

Courtesy of John Saffell.

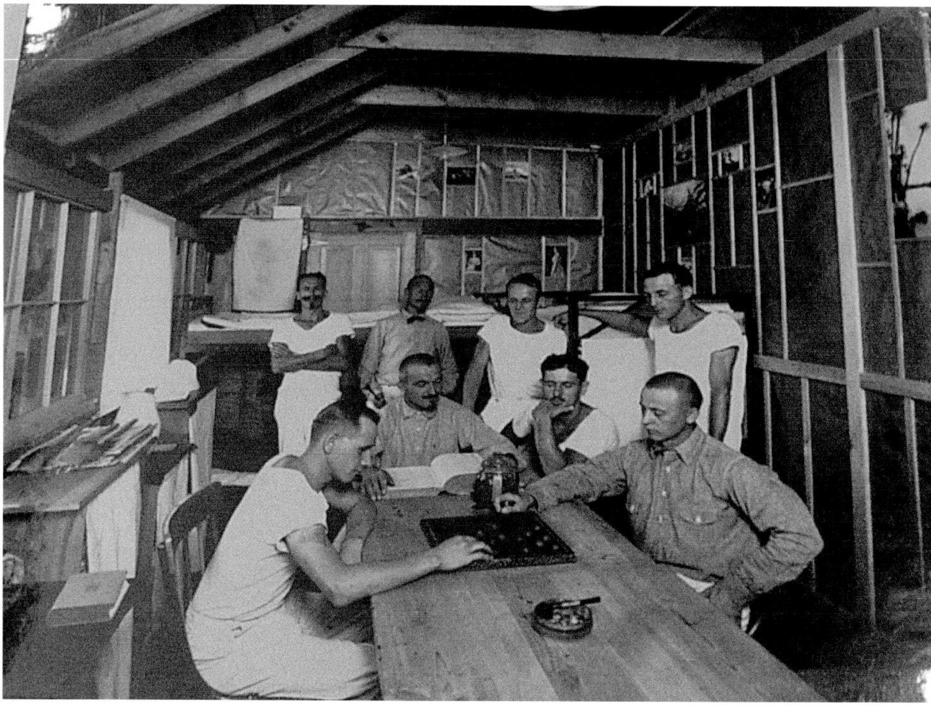

German Prisoners of War at Fort Douglas, UT, in 1917 (crews of German ships) and view of the Camp, used with permission, Utah Historical Society.

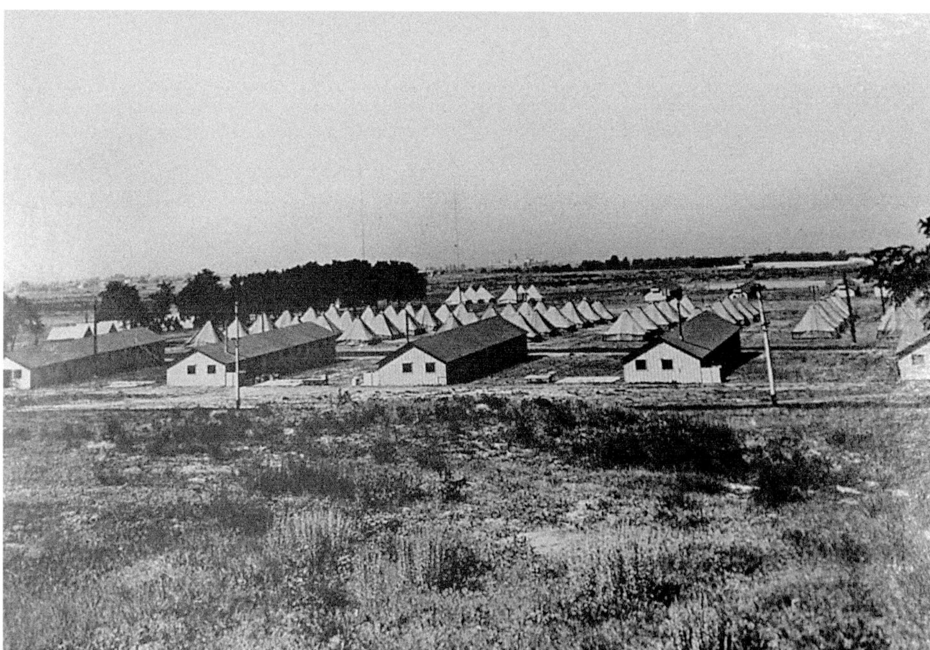

Background

By the time we entered World War II (WWII), almost the entire world was at war. This situation included large numbers of POWs which could no longer be supported by the limited resources of the British and French who captured many of them, primarily in North Africa in 1939.

The U.S. had already prepared plans for camps to house large numbers of enemy aliens, so assisting with prisoners captured by the British was easily incorporated into those general plans. It was determined early that we would not be imprisoning as many enemy aliens as first planned. The number of resident aliens who matched the original enemy alien profile was much larger than anticipated, so implementing that original plan was not possible.

During World War I (WWI), we had only 1,346 POWs held on United States soil. They were the crews of German military ships lying in U.S. ports when the war began. They were held in the same five locations as civilian enemy aliens, plus four additional locations for a total of 5,887 prisoners of war. All other prisoners of that war captured by the U.S. were held in France.

Those U.S. locations included the following:

War Prison Barracks #1—Fort McPherson, East Point, GA—100 prisoners maximum
War Prison Barracks #2—Fort Oglethorpe, Catloosa County, GA—800 prisoners maximum
War Prison Barracks #3—Fort Douglas, Salt Lake City, UT – 406 POWs and 786 enemy aliens.

On 21 March 1918, the POWs were transferred from Fort Douglas to Fort McPherson. On 19 July 1919, 108 conscientious objectors arrived at Fort Douglas from Fort Leavenworth, KS. They were housed in the compound left vacant by the POWs.
Branch camps under the camps in GA:

Camp Devens, Ayer, MA—100 prisoners maximum
Camp Grant, Rockford, IL—100 prisoners maximum
Camp Jackson, Columbia, SC—100 prisoners maximum

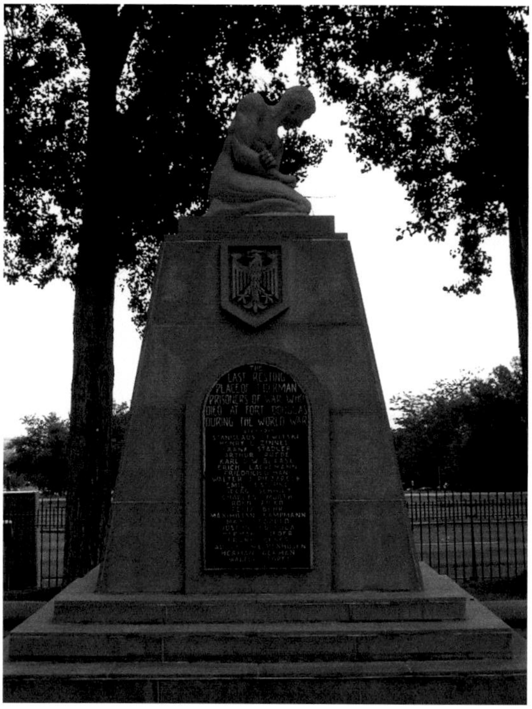

Monument to German POWs from WWI. We didn't separate the enemy aliens from the POWs, so only two of the 21 men on this list were POWs. Photo by author.

Camp Sevier, Greenville, SC—100 prisoners maximum
Camp Sherman, near Chillicothe, OH—100 prisoners maximum
Camp Wadsworth, Spartanburg, SC—100 prisoners maximum

These camps were run by the Provost Marshal General's Office (PMGO) of the U.S. Army. Initially, there were no distinctions between captured German sailors and enemy aliens rounded up from across the U.S. However, it soon became apparent that the two groups were quite different and efforts were made to put different groups into different camps.

Another camp, called an Internment Camp, was established at Hot Springs, NC, and run by the Immigration and Naturalization Service (INS). It held 2,200 Germans from commercial ships in U.S. ports when war broke out in 1914. They were placed at Hot Springs in May 1917 for the remainder of the war. Burials from this location were removed to Chattanooga National Cemetery.

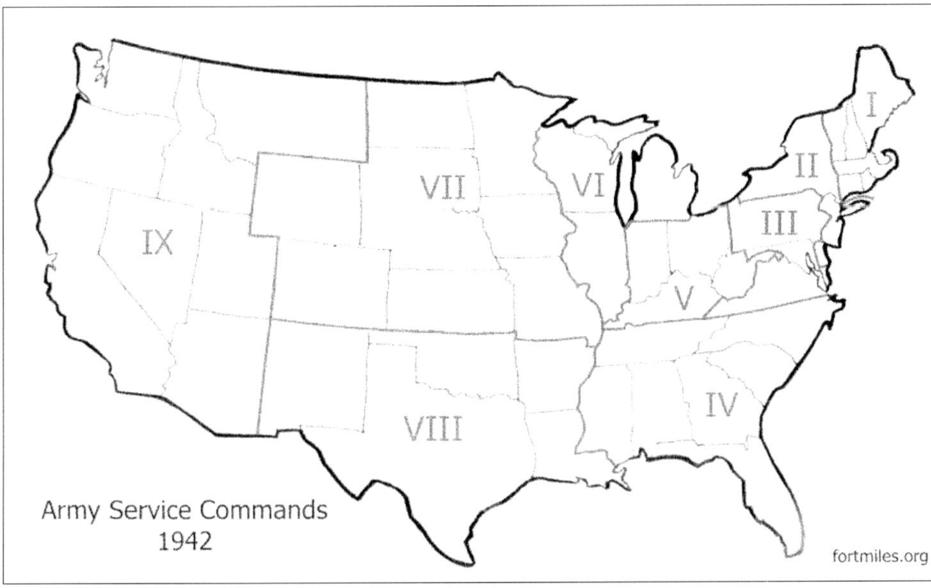

From NARA, College Park, MD.

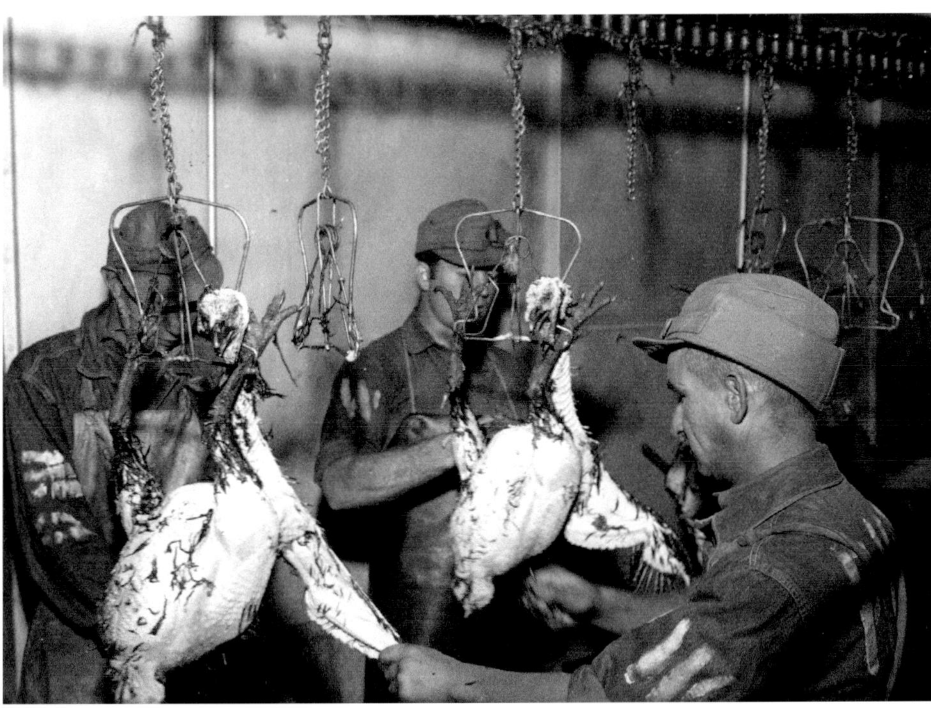

German POWs at Utah ASF Depot, courtesy of Special Collections Department, Stewart Library, Weber State University.

Preparing for War

The military headquarters/training for the 9th Service command moved inland from The Presidio of San Francisco, CA, to Fort Douglas, UT, at the end of 1941 to make it less vulnerable to a Japanese attack.

We needed:

1. Labor, since most able-bodied young men were expected in military service and efforts to recruit women into the workforce had only limited success. However, "Rosie the Riveter" became iconic and there were female pilots as well as clerks (military and civilian), nurses, and teachers; many other occupations gained workers from this effort. Those numbers decreased immediately after the war when the men returned home, but steadily increased as time passed.
2. Supplies for military troops overseas as well as both military and civilians at home including timber, cotton, tobacco, food (planting, harvesting, canning, fishing), clothing, arms and ammunition, and transportation vehicles for land, sea and air.
3. Building and maintenance of new and expanded military installations as well as roads, railways, airfields, dams, and camps for POWs and enemy aliens.

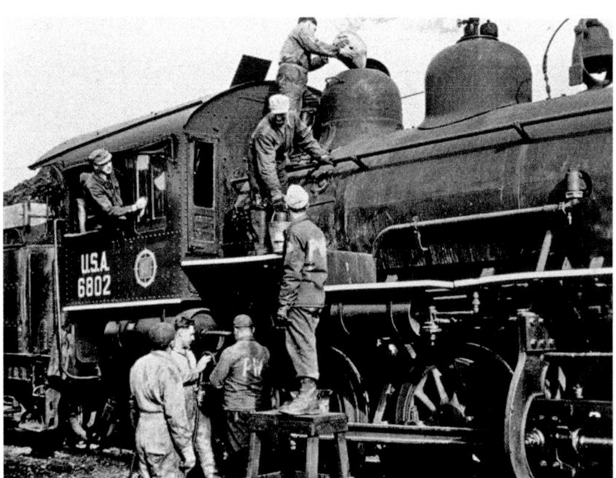

Train at Utah ASF Depot, courtesy of Special Collections Department, Stewart Library, Weber State University.

Global Situation

POWs held by the British and French were straining their limited supplies so they needed to be farmed out to other Allied nations (Algeria, Australia, Canada, Egypt, Great Britain, India, Kenya, Libya, the Middle East, South Africa, and the U.S.).

POWs were being held in the various theaters of war, but the numbers were much greater than could be used for supply and support behind combat lines. Great Britain held 23,000 German and 250,000 Italian prisoners in August 1942. Plans were made to transport them to places where their care wouldn't pull men from combat and where their labor could be used to ease shortages caused by men away from home.

Generally, ships carrying supplies and men into the European and Mediterranean theaters of war were used to transport POWs back to America, Canada, Australia, etc. While many POWs worried about getting bombed or torpedoed by their own nations, there were few incidents. The SS *Benjamin Contee* was torpedoed off the coast of Algeria on 16 August 1943 by German aircraft. The ship proceeded to Bone, to Algiers and then to Gibraltar, where emergency repairs were made, then to New York City, arriving 29 January 1944. The bodies of 36 unidentifiable Italian prisoners (900 British-held Italian prisoners had been on this ship before the attack) were removed from the most damaged part of the vessel and buried at Long Island National Cemetery.

The German POW population in the U.S. in May 1942 was only 31 with one Japanese POW. There were no Italian POWs here at that time.

The Italian POWs were captured by British, French and American troops between 1939 and 1943 in North Africa and Europe. They first arrived in the U.S. in early 1943 through the New York Port of Embarkation.

For the captured officers and naval crews, interrogation centers were their first stops in America. Fort Hunt, VA, was the first of these centers. These interrogators denied torture and criticized the Bush administration when they were honored near Alexandria as part of the U.S. Army's Freedom Team salute program in 2007. The National Park Service (NPS), particularly the George Washington Memorial Parkway which now contains the former Fort Hunt, is interviewing veterans of P.O. Box 1142 (as it was known then) to tell their story. The former interrogators include John Gunther Dean, later a career Foreign

Service Officer and ambassador to Denmark who said, "We did it with a certain amount of respect and justice." George Frenkel said, "During the many interrogations, I never laid hands on anyone." He said, "We extracted information in a battle of the wits, I'm proud to say I never compromised my humanity."

The other known interrogation center was Byron Hot Springs, CA, also known as P.O. Box 651. Following the example of the British to gain maximum cooperation with excellent living conditions, this center was used primarily for the highest-ranking officers while Fort Hunt was used primarily for naval crews. Information gained at Fort Hunt was also used later in the murder trials of naval POWs accused of murder in the camps.

A third location appearing on the camp lists as "restricted listing," the same designation as the two locations above, might be Pigeon Forge, TN, although documentation hasn't been located to confirm this location.

These three centers were run by a combination of Military Intelligence, an agency of the Adjutant General's Office (G-2) and the Office of Naval Intelligence (ONI), so are listed on PMGO lists of POW Camps as "restricted listing" camps.

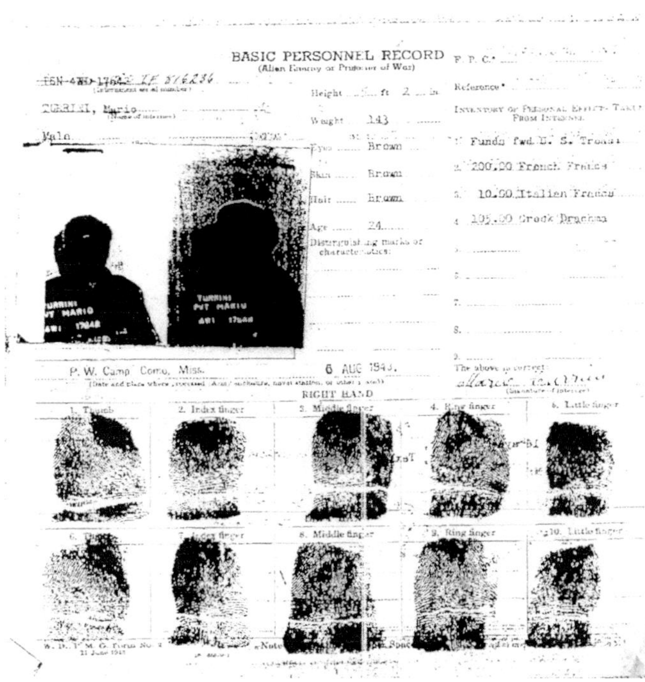

BASIC PERSONNEL RECORD
(Alien Enemy or Prisoner of War)

TURRINI, Mario

Male

Weight 143

Eyes Brown

Skin Brown

Hair Brown

Age 24

Funds fwd. U. S. Treas.

200.00 French Francs

10.00 Italian Francs

105.00 Greek Drachma

P. W. Camp Como, Miss.

6 AUG 1943

RIGHT HAND

1. Thumb

2. Index finger

3. Middle finger

4. Ring finger

5. Little finger

8. Middle finger

9. Ring finger

10. Little finger

This ID card for Mario Turrini was created at Camp Como, MS. Note that the ID # was crossed out when they realized he already had a POW number assigned by the British who had originally captured him. In the far right column you can see that he had coins from France from his service in Tunisia, plus coins from Italy from his Italian Army pay, plus coins from Greece, his last duty station before Tunisia. These documents are courtesy of his son, Marcello, who lives in Italy.

This card for Mario Turrini was created at Camp Ruston, LA, his location after processing at Camp Como. It shows that in May 1944 he was transferred to Camp Hereford, TX. This is part of the sorting process and he was categorized as not cooperative since he didn't sign up to be a co-belligerent in the Italian Service Units (ISU) after the fall of Mussolini. In September 1944, he was transferred to the Seattle Port of Entry, particularly Fort Lawton from which he sailed two weeks later for duty at POW Camp APO 950, AKA Fort Armstrong, Honolulu, HI. The Italian prisoners weren't sure where they were going and there was unrest among the African American units at Fort Lawton, so when one of the Italians committed suicide, three African American soldiers were convicted of murder. They weren't cleared until 2005, primarily because of the book *On American Soil* by Jack Hamman.

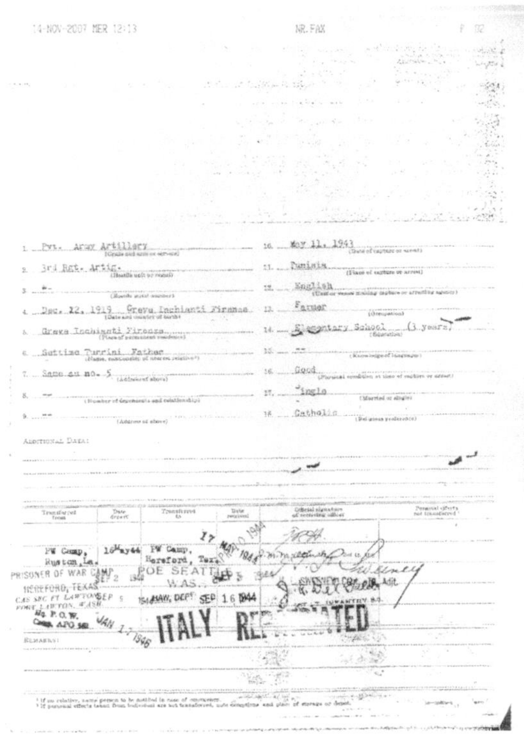

1. Pvt. Army Artillery (Grade and arm or service)
2. 3rd Rgt. Artig. (Hostile unit or vessel)
3. -- (Hostile serial number)
4. Dec. 22, 1919 Greve Inchianti Firenze (Date and country of birth)
5. Greve Inchianti Firenze (Place of permanent residence)
6. Settimo Turrini Father (Name, relationship of nearest relative)
7. Same as no. 5 (Address of above)
8. -- (Number of dependents and relationship)
9. -- (Address of above)
10. May 11, 1943 (Date of capture or arrest)
11. Tunisia (Place of capture or arrest)
12. English (Unit or vessel making capture or arresting agency)
13. Farmer (Occupation)
14. Elementary School (3 years) (Education)
15. -- (Knowledge of languages)
16. Good (Physical condition at time of capture or arrest)
17. Single (Married or single)
18. Catholic (Religious preference)

Additional Data:

Transferred from	Date depart	Transferred to	Date received	Official signature of receiving officer	Personal effects not transferred
PW Camp, Ruston, La.	16 May 44	PW Camp, Hereford, Tex.	17 May 1944		
Prisoner of War Camp Hereford, Texas	Sep 2 1944	POE Seattle Was.	Sep 5 1944		
Cas Sec Ft Lawton Fort Lawton, Wash.	Sep 9 1944	Haw. Dept	Sep 16 1944		
Hq. P.O.W. Camp APO 960	Jan 17 1946	Italy			

Remarks:

ITALY REPATRIATED

[1] If no relative, name person to be notified in case of emergency.
[2] If personal effects taken from individual are not transferred, note exceptions and place of storage or deposit.

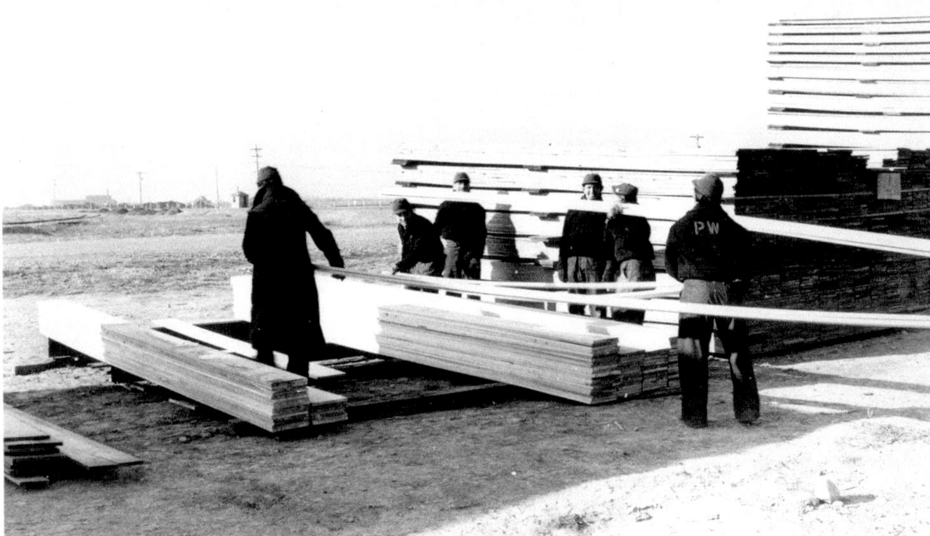

Construction at Utah ASF Depot, courtesy of Special Collections Department, Stewart Library, Weber State University.

Planning and Building the Camps

Initially, enemy alien camps were planned for 100,000 internees. However, even after it was determined that original parameters for designating enemy aliens as potential threats were too broad and couldn't be implemented because of the vast numbers of people involved, the camps under construction were re-purposed as POW camps. They expected to fill them with POWs already captured by the British, about 100,000.

Lessons learned in WWI led to the separation of POWs (run by the PMGO of the Army) and enemy aliens (run by INS within the Department of Justice [DOJ]). Also in the wake of WWI were the agreements made at the Geneva Convention in 1929. It was determined that the U.S. would (usually) follow such agreements not only because of the legal obligations, but also in hopes of reciprocal treatment by our enemies.

Among those soldiers captured in German uniform were men who considered themselves another nationality, such as Austrian, Czech, Swiss, Italian, Russian, Mongol, Hungarian, Romanian, and more. Among those captured in Japanese uniform were Koreans. Among those captured in Italian uniforms were Slavs (present day Croatia, Bosnia, and Slovenia), Albanians, and Ethiopians. It was quickly learned that these groups needed to be separated in the POW camps both at home and abroad. In many of these groups were those who claimed U.S. citizenship.

One of the POW camps had previously been used as WWI POW camp: Fort Douglas, UT. Some were already military installations, like Fort Jay, NY. Some were former Civilian Conservation Corps (CCC) camps, like Fort Hunt, VA. Many were new purchases, like Camp Monticello, AR.

There were several potential standard plans, adapted to different climates and geographical considerations, but ultimately, each camp was unique in its layout due to geography and transportation infrastructure. In addition to building barracks, mess halls, warehouses, administrative buildings, and a hospital, the first commanding officer of the Utah ASF Depot POW camp, UT, designated 50 acres nearby to grow crops to help feed the POWs. The crop yield was so bountiful it was shared with the Depot cafeteria, the Depot quartermaster, Bushnell General Hospital (in Brigham City), and the Ogden Air Service Command at nearby Hill Field. A similar assortment of buildings and garden area was described at other locations.

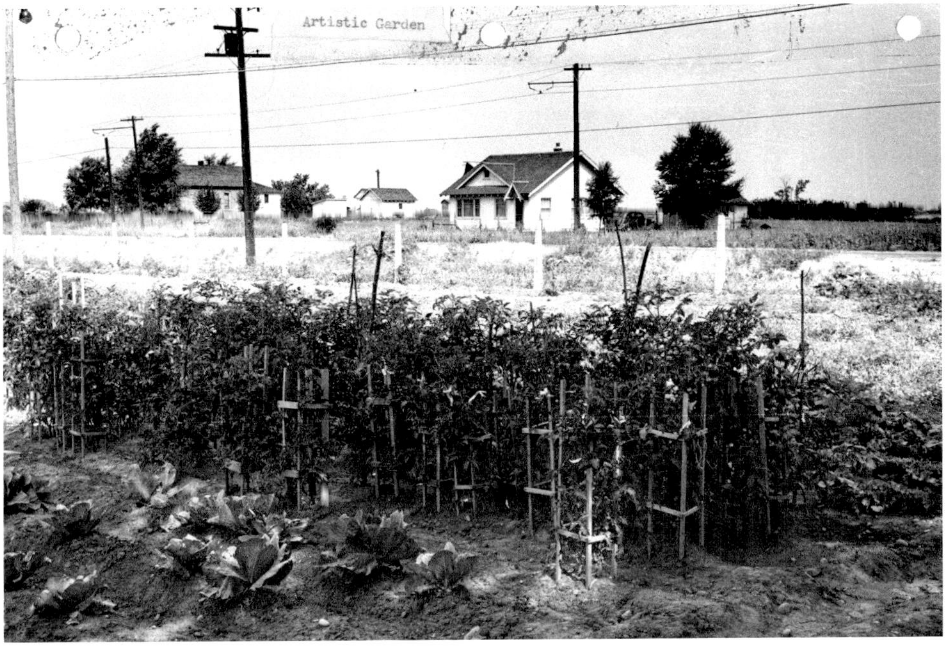

Garden at Utah ASF Depot, courtesy of Special Collections Department, Stewart Library, Weber State University.

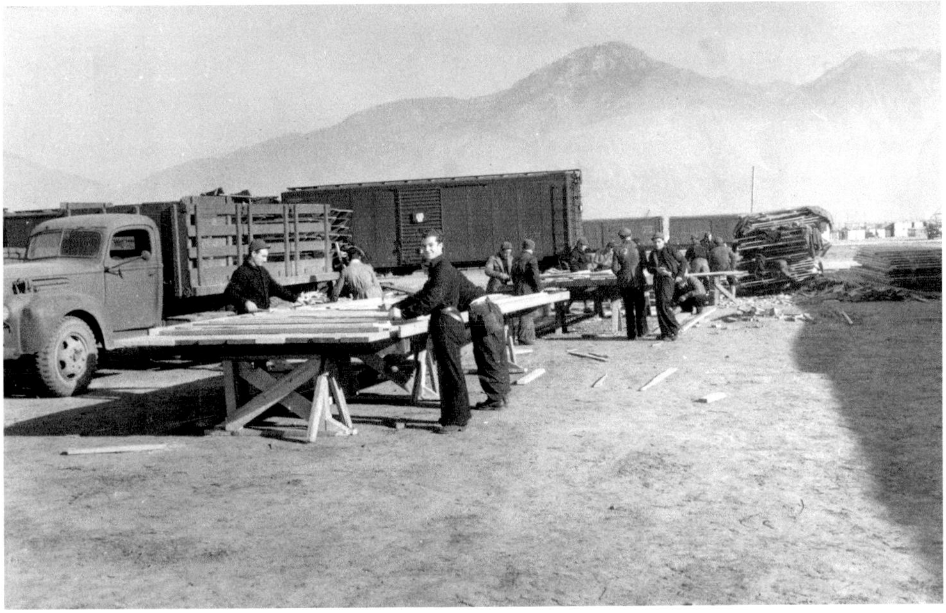

Italian Prisoners of War in freight yard at Ogden Depot, courtesy of courtesy of Special Collections Department, Stewart Library, Weber State University.

Managing the Camps

Security was a primary concern. Guards were a combination of military (often older men and wounded combat veterans) and civilian. Sometimes long-lasting friendships developed between the guards and the POWs they watched, particularly among the interpreters.

In a successful effort to conserve manpower, it was the experience at Utah ASF Depot, UT, that one woman with a dog could patrol the same area as two men.

The POW work details were supervised by guards armed with carbines and rifles. Originally, the ratio was one guard to ten POWs, but over time diminished to one guard to 32 prisoners. When American Army personnel wasn't available, the commander could supply guards from other sources. Handcuffing or abuse was forbidden. Each of the guard towers in the compound was occupied by a guard equipped with machine guns.

Sometimes the U.S. Army translators were also guards, like Thomas M. Todaro, who worked at Camp Monticello and later at Fort Leonard Wood, MO. Translators (usually U.S. Military) were assigned to camps. However, U.S. Military translators for Italian Service Units (ISU) were assigned to the units which moved from camp to camp as needed to provide services.

The POWs were soon discovered to be an uneasy, even dangerous, mix of several nationalities, languages, and ideologies, regardless of their uniform. They were then segregated by nationality and politics and rank. In many camps, the officers were simply held in a separate compound from the enlisted, as directed by the Geneva Convention. However, compounds at Camps Beale, Blanding, McCain, and Papago Park were designated for German Naval crews. Camp Alva was for Nazis. Camps Blanding, Campbell, and Camp Devens were anti-Nazi camps. Camps Hereford, Monticello, and Weingarten were for Italian fascists. These divisions into Nazi and anti-Nazi were based on judgments made by G-2, the Army Intelligence unit.

The generalities don't take into account transfers from camp to camp that were frequent and based on additional factors, such as work, health, and relationships. Most POWs didn't fall into the above categories; they were young men who grew up in societies with mandatory youth groups and mandatory military service.

After initial interrogation, the German generals were placed at Camps Clinton and Dermott while Italian generals and officers were at Camp Monticello. Additional German officers were held at Crossville.

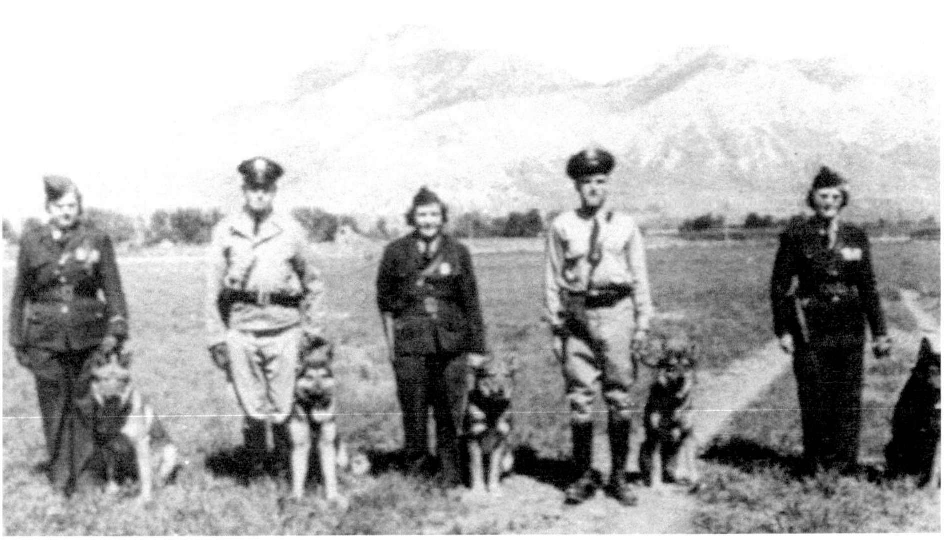

Utah ASF Depot guard photos, courtesy of Special Collections Department, Stewart Library, Weber State University.

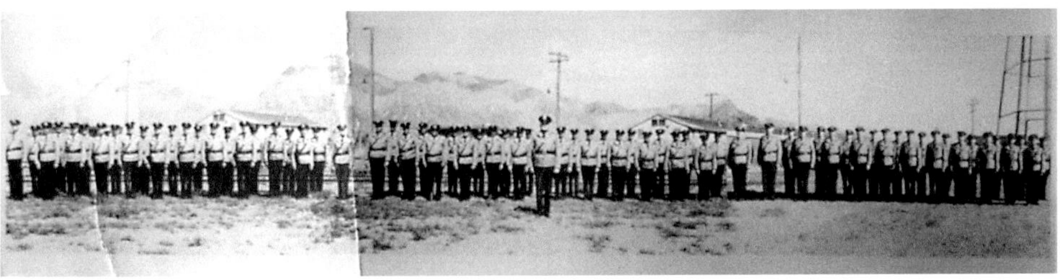

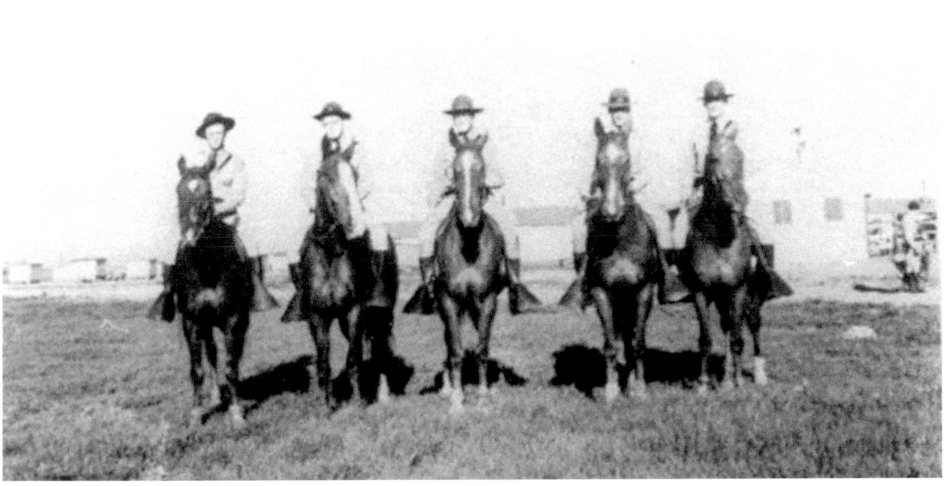

Guards (previous photo), security on horseback at Utah ASF Depot, courtesy of Special Collections Department, Stewart Library, Weber State University.

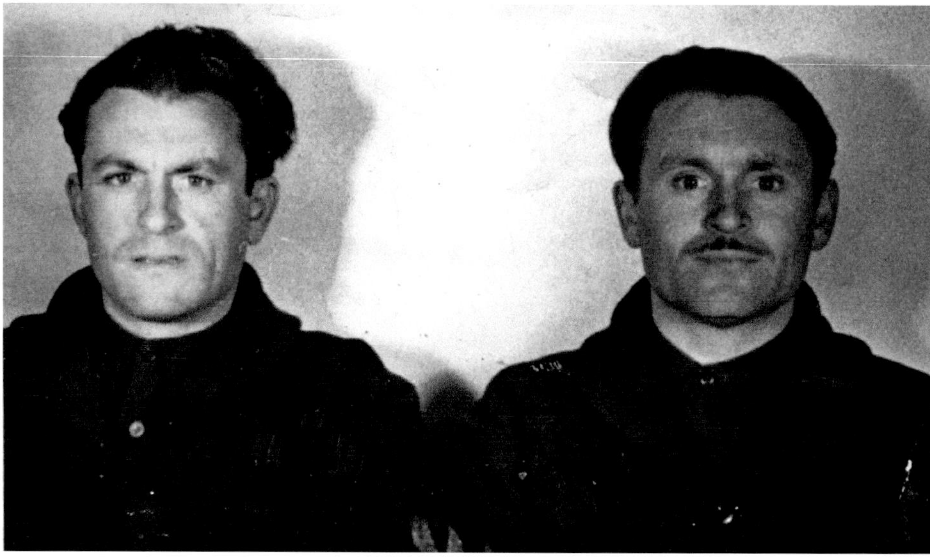

Orazio and Angelo Vecchio, brothers and Italian Prisoners at ASF Depot Ogden, Courtesy of Orazio's grandson, Orazio Vecchio, living in Italy.

G-2 interviewed these officers; however, the highest-ranking officer in these interrogation teams was a major, so not qualified to deal with an officer of higher rank. Consequently, cursory and sometimes erroneous conclusions were drawn, heavily influenced by other high-ranking officers who were invited to participate.

A glaring example is the input of Italian General Trezzani who used the opportunity to cast doubt (and worse, call another general a Nazi). He used this ploy on officers of similar rank to promote himself with the Americans. He used it to great advantage to become the head of the Italian Service Units (ISU) in the U.S. and later in charge of rebuilding the Italian Army in post-war Italy.

Additionally, Italian Royalists and career army were considered fascist while German career army were consider Nazi, simply for participating in youth groups (required) or in support of Franco (military service) in Spain. There was so much more to the story.

Public opinion was most loudly expressed by those with the greatest fear of enemy camps in their towns, or by those who hoped to profit from the use of POW labor in their businesses. Most Americans viewed the new camps with caution, but acceptance, and gradually came to appreciate the additional civilian jobs and affordable labor source. Some even developed friendships which lasted long after the war ended.

Each prisoner was processed either when captured or when they arrived in the U.S. This process included searching, delousing, disinfecting, fumigation, bathing, registration, clothing issue, quartering, and medical inspection.

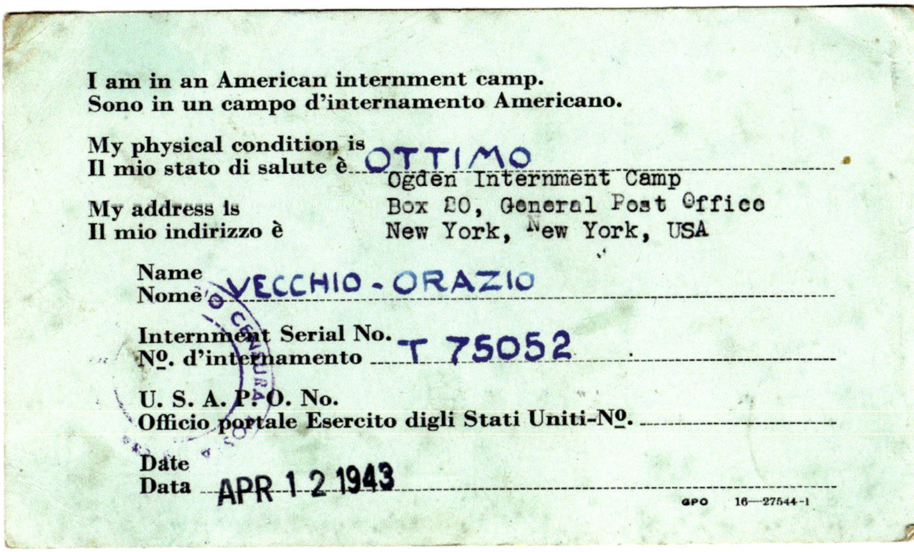
I am in an American internment camp.
Sono in un campo d'internamento Americano.

My physical condition is
Il mio stato di salute è OTTIMO

My address is
Il mio indirizzo è
Ogden Internment Camp
Box 20, General Post Office
New York, New York, USA

Name
Nome VECCHIO - ORAZIO

Internment Serial No.
N°. d'internamento T 75052

U. S. A. P. O. No.
Officio portale Esercito digli Stati Uniti-N°.

Date
Data APR 12 1943

GPO 16—27544-1

Standard POW form, filled out for Orazio Vecchio, courtesy of his grandson, Orazio Vecchio.

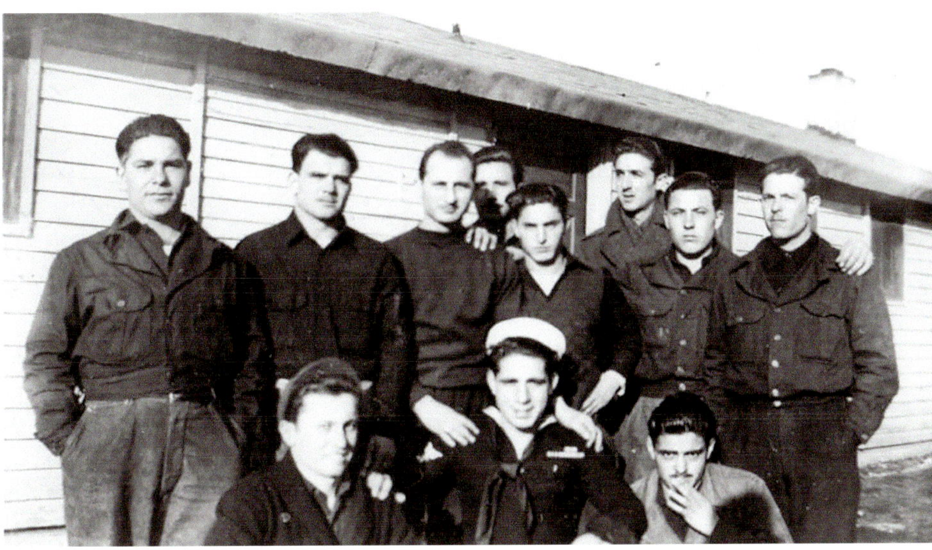

Photo of Giovanni D'Onofrio (3rd from left) and friends at Ogden Depot, courtesy of his children, Vincent, Orazio, and Janice.

Life in the Camps

The maximum number of German POWs held in the continental U.S. was 371,683 in May 1945. Italian POWs (continental U.S.) reached a maximum of 51,156 in November 1944. Japanese POWs (continental U.S.) reached a maximum of 5,413 in August 1945. There were POW camps in every state except Vermont, plus the territories of Hawaii and Alaska.

The POWs were placed into companies of 250 men each, eight companies to a compound (2,000 men), with two compounds at Ogden ASF Depot in 1943. Later, one compound at Ogden ASF Depot was composed of Italian Service Units while the other housed German POWs who were willing to work there. They were the first camp to work the two groups together, with Germans supervising Italians and the opposite.

Each base camp had a station hospital, staffed by both Americans and POWs. Utah ASF Depot station hospital had 100 beds. Since many POWs arrived in poor health due to long imprisonment and poor diet (both before and after imprisonment), that hospital admitted over 2,000 men by June 1944 after opening only eighteen months earlier.

Housing and furnishings at first met, and then exceeded the Geneva Convention requirements. Since the camps were in different locations, some utilized barracks, some hutments (smaller housing units) while the temporary and seasonal camps often used tents. The Geneva Convention required mattresses only for officers. Eventually, most permanent camps had mattresses, pillows, and pillow cases on iron and wooden beds for enlisted men as well as officers.

General hospitals, run by the Surgeon General of Army Service Forces (ASF), were in each region, utilizing a POW wing to facilitate security. In 1944, they became more specialized to receive all patients from theaters of operations, plus patients needing specialized treatment in the zone of interior.

Those station hospitals with airfields were overseen by the Air Surgeon of the Army Air Force (AAF). In 1944, regional hospitals (a new designation), station hospitals, and convalescent centers were now run by both the ASF and AAF. The regional hospitals were to serve as general hospitals for zone of interior patients. These designations are rarely mentioned in the population lists in the National Archives.

The station hospitals were generally staffed with an American officer of the Medical Corps and 3 POW attendants with medical training. The surgical staff included an American

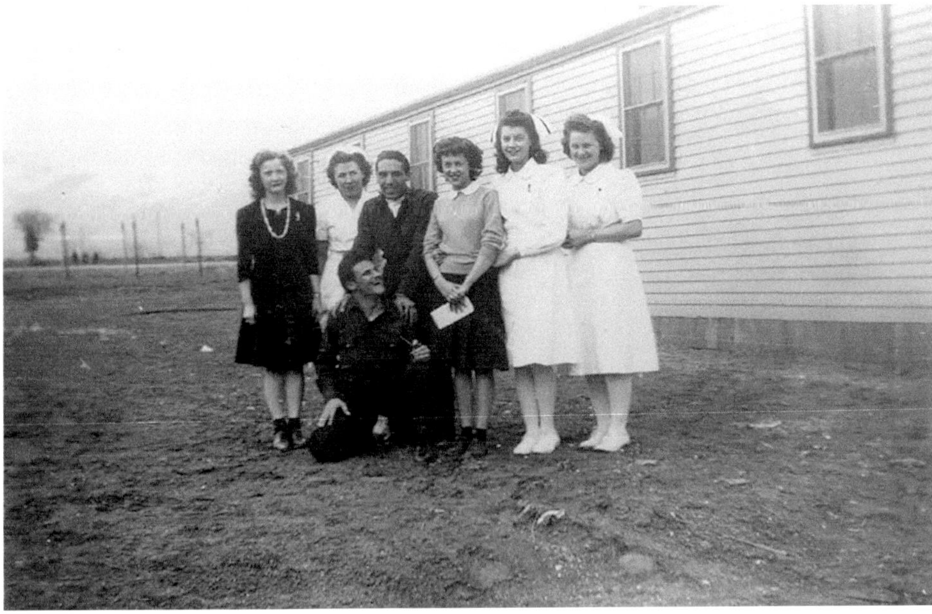

Ogden Depot Hospital, courtesy of Special Collections Department, Stewart Library, Weber State University.

Medical Officer, a nurse, an enlisted man, and three POW attendants with medical training. POWs also served as lab technicians. The hospital mess was under the mess officer with a civilian nurse and a mess sergeant. It was staffed by two Army mess sergeants, one POW mess sergeant and four POW cooks. Provisions were made for special diets.

Mental patients in Utah were sent to Bushnell General Hospital, UT, while extreme cases were sent to Mason General Hospital, NY. Dental care was also provided at the station hospital for the POWs treating abscesses, and doing extractions, fillings, and gum treatments. At Utah ASF Depot, over 17,000 dental cases were treated during the year of 1943-1944.

Upon arrival, the POWs were issued clothing and blankets which were maintained and replaced as needed. The Red Cross in New York was issuing two pairs of blankets per man and a uniform that might be the dark blue with white PW lettering, or an old U.S. Army uniform, plus the uniform he arrived wearing. Not many had overcoats; some came with English overcoats, black with a black diamond on the back.

The POWs were supposed to be adequately, comfortably, and properly clothed in accordance with the climate conditions in which they lived and worked. The War Department later determined that dark blue was a preferable color since it would not be mistaken for the American khaki. They were also provided with woolen underwear, cotton underwear, woolen socks and cotton socks, woolen shirts and cotton shirts, two pairs of

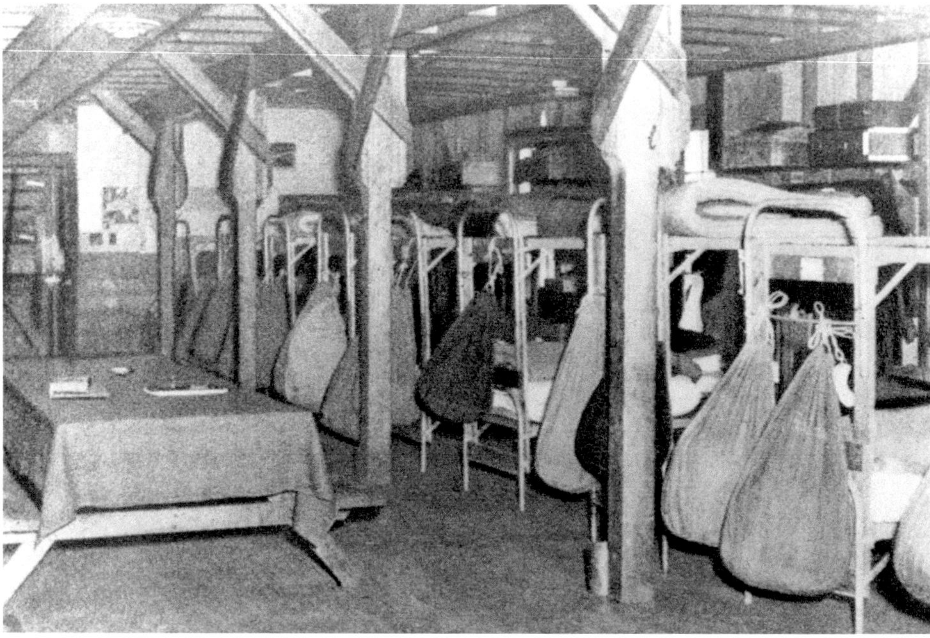

Barracks at Hill Field, used with permission, Utah Historical Society.

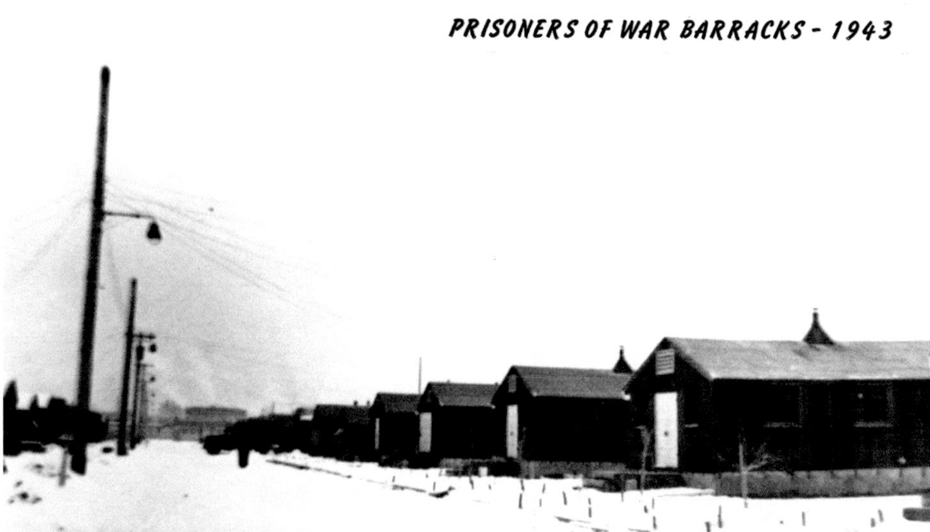

Barracks at Utah ASF Depot, courtesy of Special Collections Department, Stewart Library, Weber State University.

trousers in either wool or denim, two cotton coats in wool or khaki, a wool overcoat, a raincoat, woolen caps and hats, cotton hats and caps, shoes and overshoes, gloves, and two heavy woolen blankets. When an item wore out, it was immediately replaced. The clothing was class X or class B, American issue.

Some camps had laundry facilities with machines while some had wash rooms where laundry was done by hand.

Education included language classes, history classes, and clerical and equipment training. Supplies were provided for many art projects and newsletter production.

Newspapers were produced by the prisoners at most of the larger camps. There is a collection of Italian POW newsletters at Utah State University. There is a large collection of German POW newsletters at the Library of Congress. Many of these newsletters can be found at local colleges and historical societies.

Their food was the equivalent of that issued to American servicemen (type A field ration), according to the Geneva Convention, although substitutions were made to recognize ethnic preferences. The Italian POWs had an increase in rice, spaghetti, macaroni, noodles, and pasta with decreases in meats and baked beans. Germans had an increase in potatoes and a decrease in beans. Meals were served three times daily. Special menus were prepared on Thanksgiving, Christmas, New Year's and other holidays. For many prisoners, these rations exceeded their military experience. The average prisoner at Utah ASF Depot gained fifteen pounds.

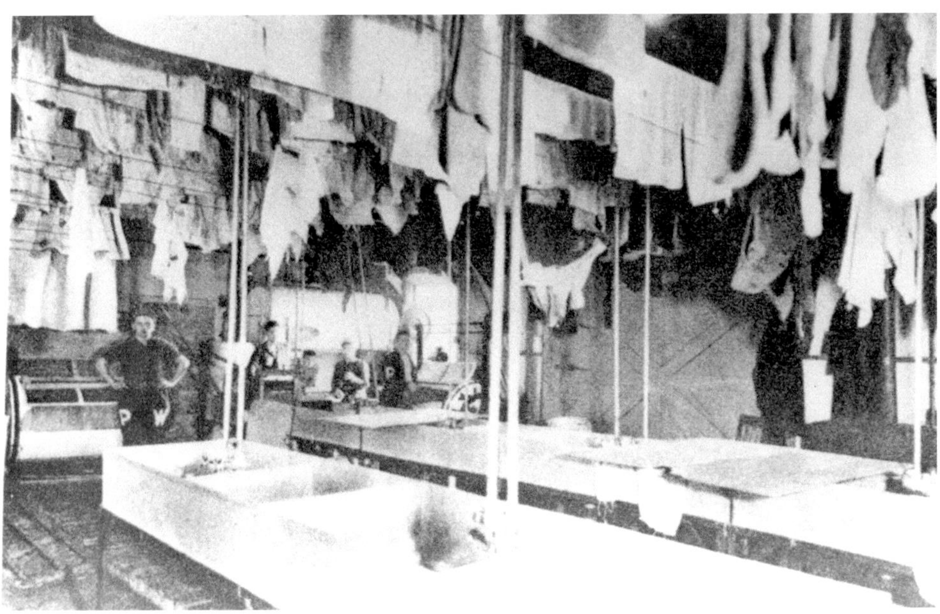

Hill Field German POW Laundry, used with permission, Utah Historical Society.

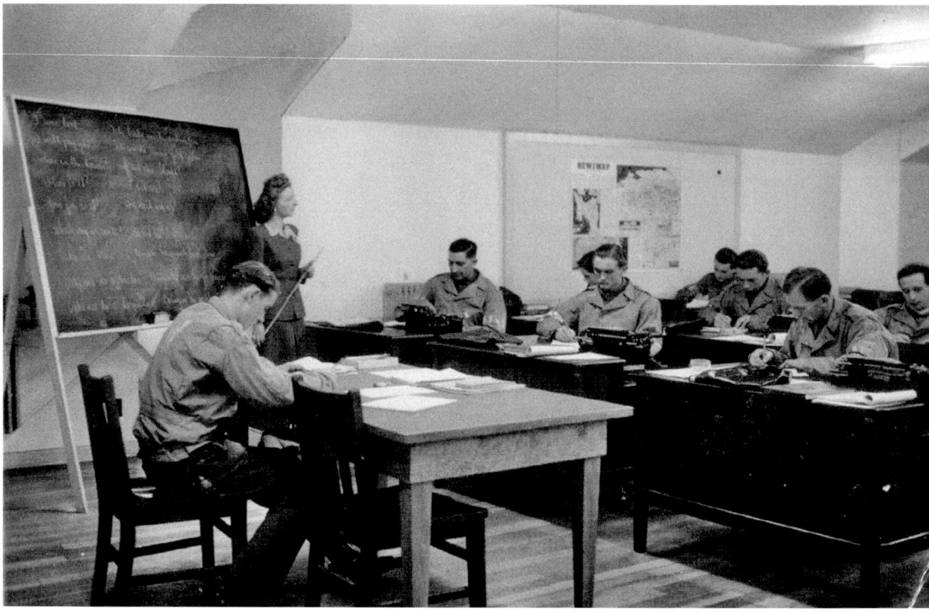

German Typing Class at Utah ASF Depot, courtesy of Special Collections Department, Stewart Library, Weber State University.

The POWs were their own cooks and bakers, paid the same wage as those working in all occupations both in and outside of the camps. However, each camp commander had some autonomy and after the liberation of concentration camps in Germany, some camps restricted food allowances for POWs well below Geneva Convention (Hereford, TX, is infamous for its dietary cuts in 1945).

Many services were available for POWs; some were in accord with the Geneva Convention, while some were additional benefits. They included canteens, camp stores where a POW could spend the pay (in coupons) he'd earned working on such items as beer, cigarettes, and gold jewelry (high quality necklaces, wedding rings, and rosaries were in high demand by the Italian POWs at Utah ASF Depot). The profits from the sales were returned to the POWs in the form of free beer, cigarettes, and theater tickets.

Some POW photos show the decorations (pin-ups) in their personal areas. These could include small pictures of national leaders and flags and emblems, but large displays were limited to funerals and religious services.

Recreation supplies were provided for many sports, although soccer was most popular. Other equipment included baseball, softball, basketball, football, boxing, volleyball, croquet, horse shoes, badminton, and table tennis. Many game sets were also provided for the POWs including dominoes, Chinese checkers, checkers, backgammon, India, bingo, chess, playing cards, etc. The POW often constructed their own volleyball courts, baseball diamonds, and soccer fields.

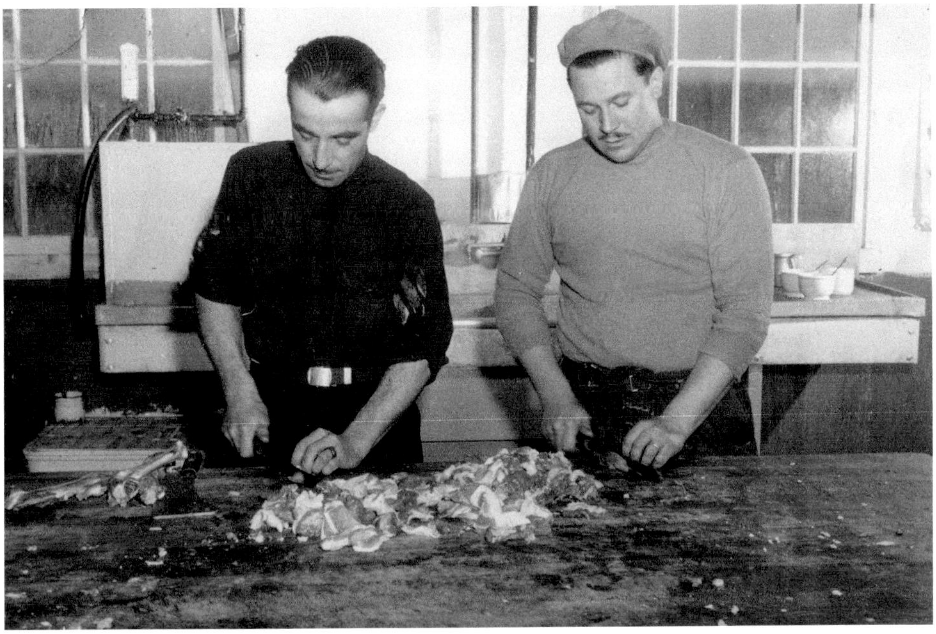

Italian POW cooks at Utah ASF Depot Courtesy of Special Collections Department, Stewart Library, Weber State University.

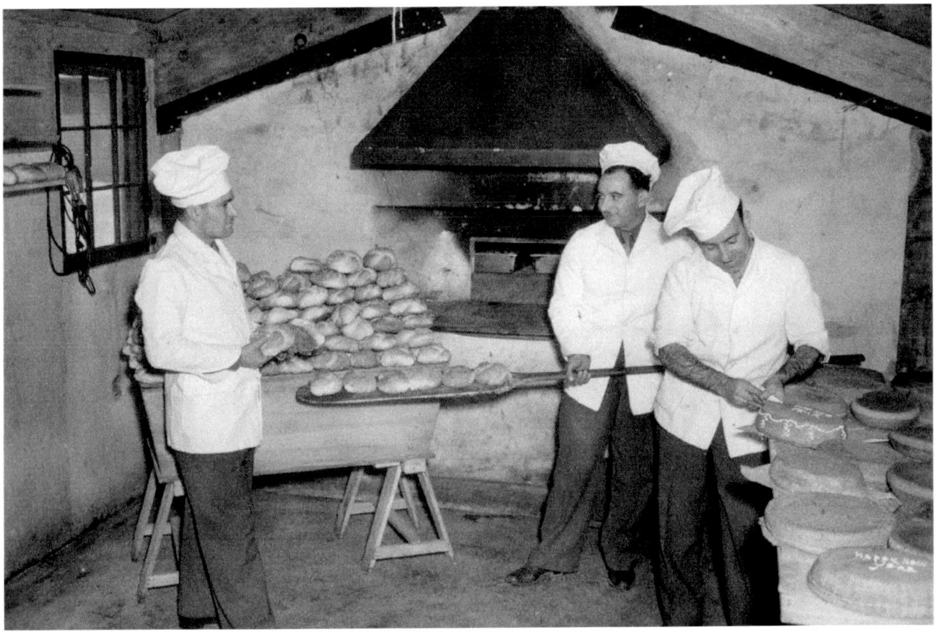

Ogden Depot Italian POW Bakery, courtesy of Special Collections Department, Stewart Library, Weber State University.

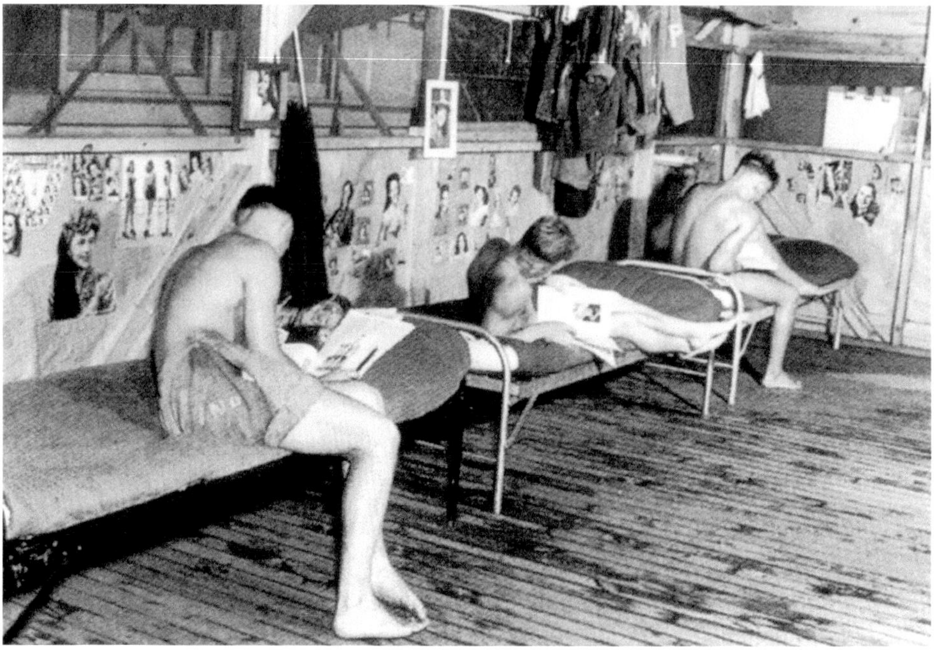

Barracks at Camp Atterbury, courtesy of Alessandro de Gaetano.

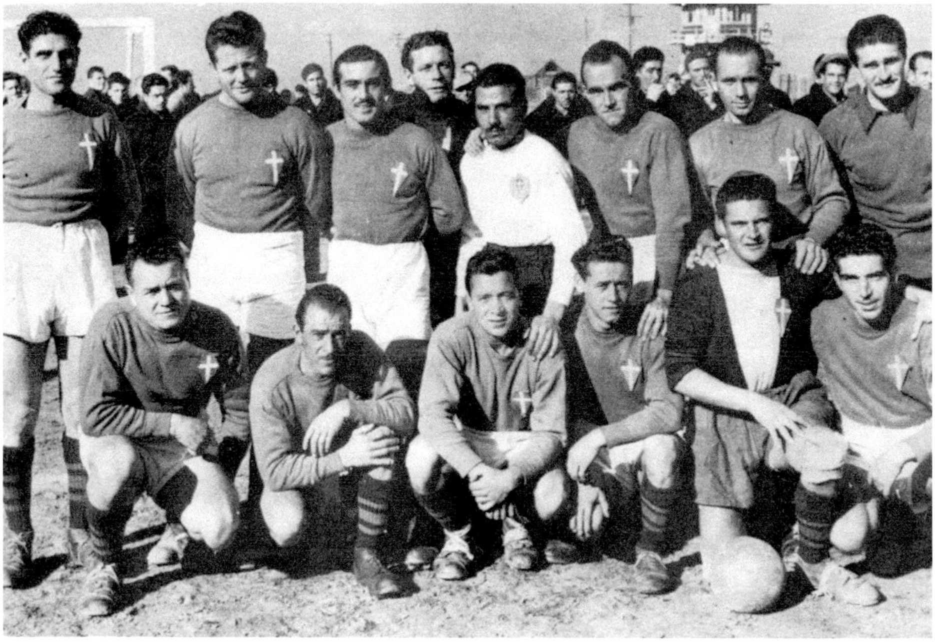

Italian POW Soccer Team, Ogden Depot, courtesy of Special Collections Department, Stewart Library, Weber State University.

POW contacts with families and others included inspection visits from the Red Cross, YMCA, Swiss government, and other welfare organizations. Each POW was permitted two letters and one postcard per week, written in ink (not pencil). Also, when necessary, one business letter per week was allowed. Special stationary was provided, so they were limited to the number of lines on the forms. Free mailing was applied to all letters, postcards, and parcels less than four pounds, addressed to or sent by a POW through the U.S. Postal Service. Each POW was also allowed, at his own expense, one prepaid cable or telegram per month. In the event of a serious emergency (death or serious illness), and at the discretion of the Base Commander, more than one per month could be sent.

Incoming mail for Italian POWs from relatives in the U.S. was enormous. In two or three months alone, 300-500 packages were received at Utah ASF Depot. The POWs sent many gifts to their relatives in this country and to those outside the continental U.S. Correspondence to POWs was permitted from anyone. However, POWs could only write to and receive packages from family members (wife, grandparents, parents, siblings, aunts, uncles, children, nieces, and nephews). They received packages also only from family listed above.

Most camps had bands and/or orchestras made up of their POW population. At Ogden, UT, concerts were held once a week. The orchestra also played for stage shows and gave monthly concerts. Many instruments were provided by the Catholic church, others were loaned by the Depot Quartermaster. At some camps, the local schools and communities provided instruments.

The ISU band played for dances each week, both at the Camp and at St. Joseph's Catholic Church in Ogden. The dances were a good place to meet the local girls. The POWs were taken to the church by bus from the camp. Separate dances on different nights were held for officers and enlisted POWs to adhere to the Geneva Convention.

Religion was also a part of camp life. At first, religious services at Ogden, UT, were held in the open with an improvised pulpit. Later, a recreation hall was used part time for morning mass. An empty barrack was utilized as a regular chapel for weekdays. Later, the old Compound One Headquarters building became the main chapel and accommodated about 300 POWs for daily mass. When Compound Two was activated, one of its recreational halls was provided for chapel functions and accommodated about 700. This camp was Italian, so only Catholic services were required. The hospital also held mass on Sunday. When the camp opened a German compound, a Lutheran minister provided services on Sunday in addition to the Catholic services for the German POWs.

While POWs weren't allowed to donate blood (prohibited by the PMGO and Geneva Convention), they were allowed to make voluntary contributions to specific organizations, such as the Red Cross and the YMCA. A minor political group at Utah ASF Depot, the Republicans, collected $80 for war bonds, offered to donate blood, and offered the money to the Infantile Paralysis Fund because they believed it was a good cause.

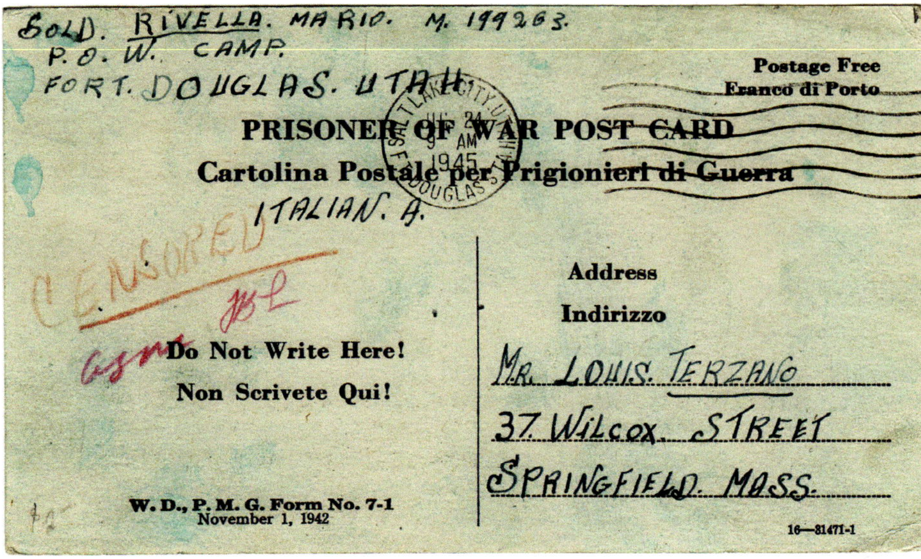

SOLD. RIVELLA. MARIO. M. 199263.
P.O.W. CAMP.
FORT. DOUGLAS. UTAH.
ITALIAN. A.

Postage Free
Franco di Porto

PRISONER OF WAR POST CARD
Cartolina Postale per Prigionieri di Guerra

CENSORED

Do Not Write Here!
Non Scrivete Qui!

W. D., P. M. G. Form No. 7-1
November 1, 1942

Address
Indirizzo

MR. LOUIS. TERZANO
37 WILCOX. STREET
SPRINGFIELD. MASS.

16—81471-1

POW Postcard courtesy of Dennis H. Pack.

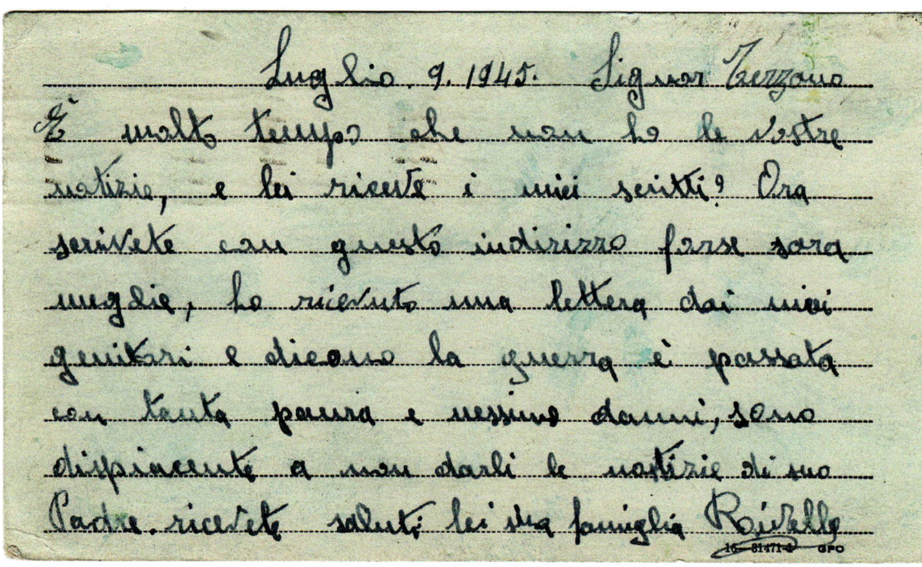

Luglio 9. 1945. Signor Terzano
È molto tempo che non ho le vostre
notizie, e lei riceve i miei scritti? Ora
scrivete con questo indirizzo forse sarà
meglio, ho ricevuto una lettera dai miei
genitori e dicono la guerra è passata
con tanta paura e nessun danni, sono
dispiacente a non darli le notizie di suo
Padre. ricevete saluti lei sua famiglia Rivella

16—81471-1 GPO

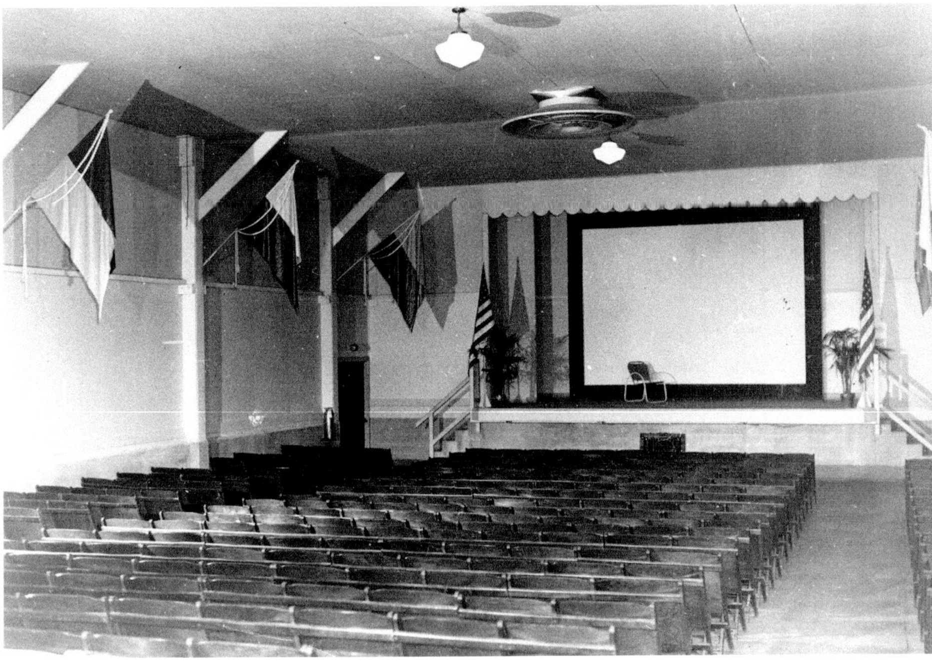

Italian POW Theater at Utah ASF Depot.

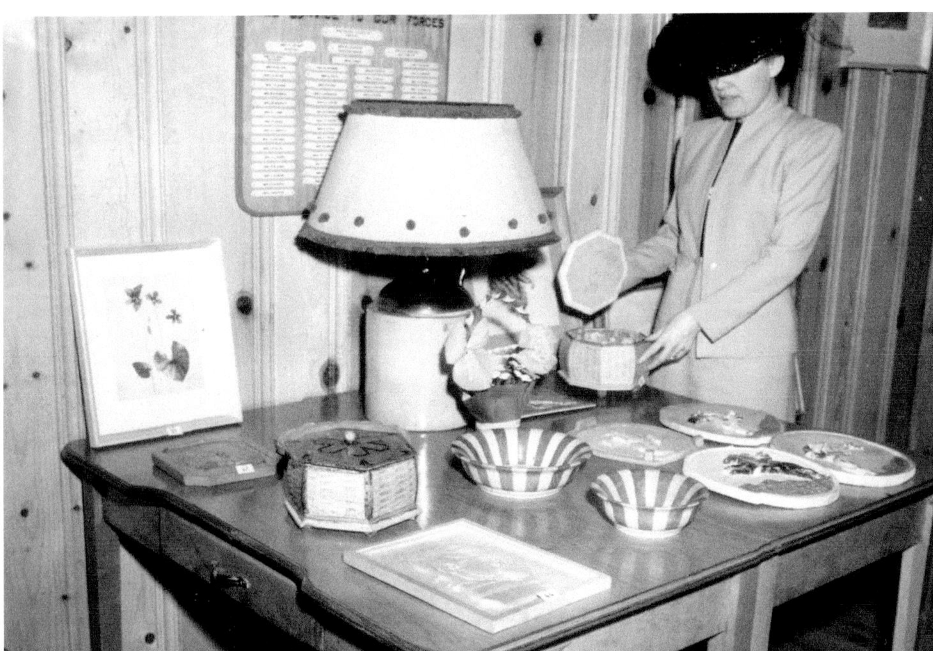

German POW art show, courtesy of Special Collections Department, Stewart Library, Weber State University.

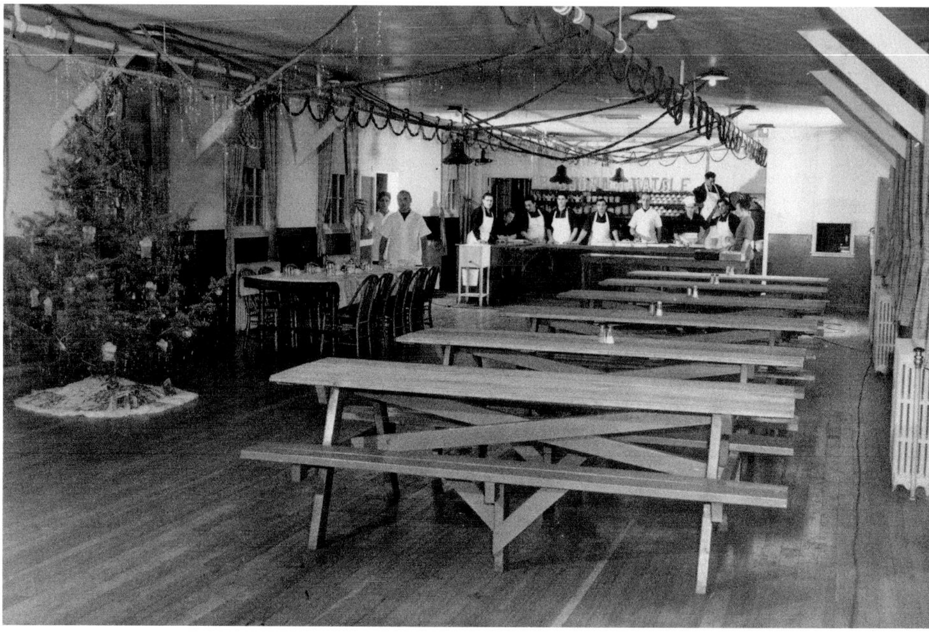

Utah ASF Mess at Christmas and ISU party, courtesy of Special Collections Department, Stewart Library, Weber State University.

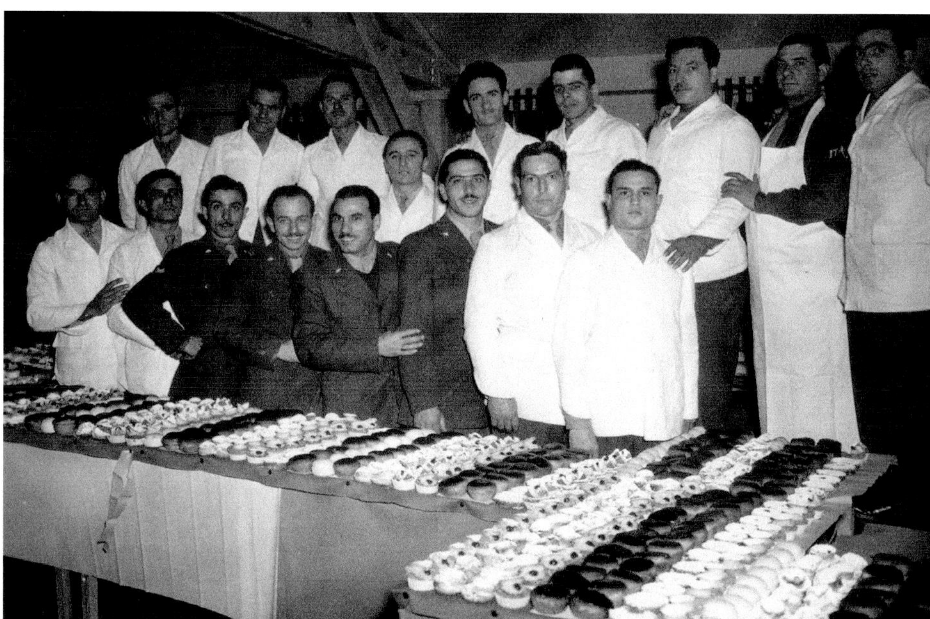

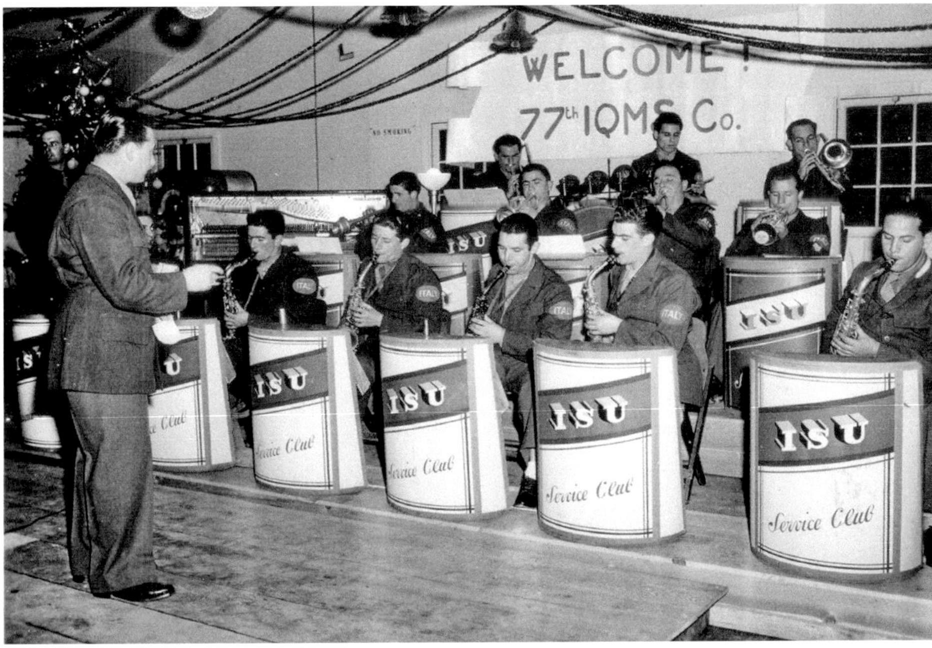

ISU Band at Utah USF Depot, courtesy of Andrea Selmi, son of Carlo Selmi, clarinet player in this band (3rd from left), living in Italy.

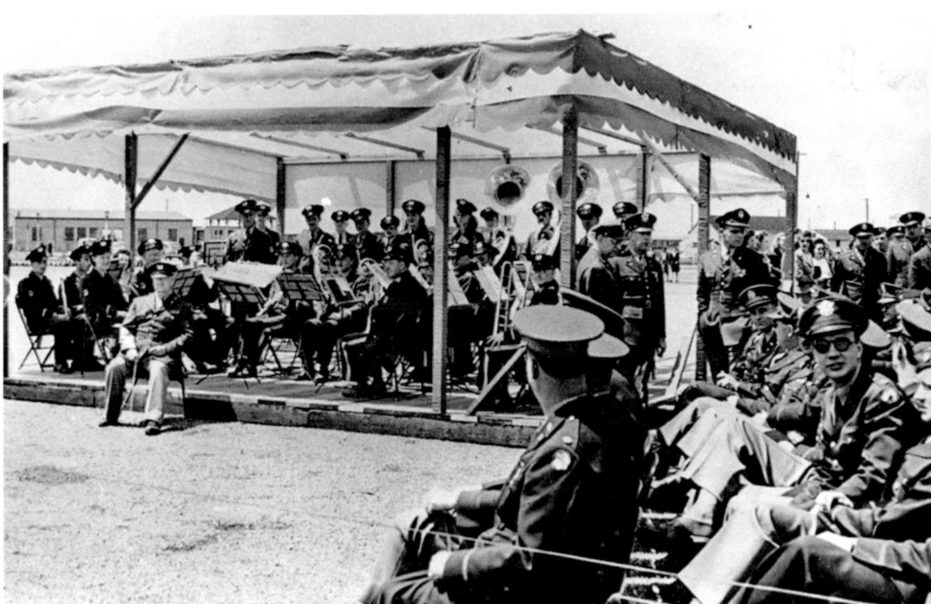

Band concert at Ogden Depot, photo courtesy of Andrea Selmi.

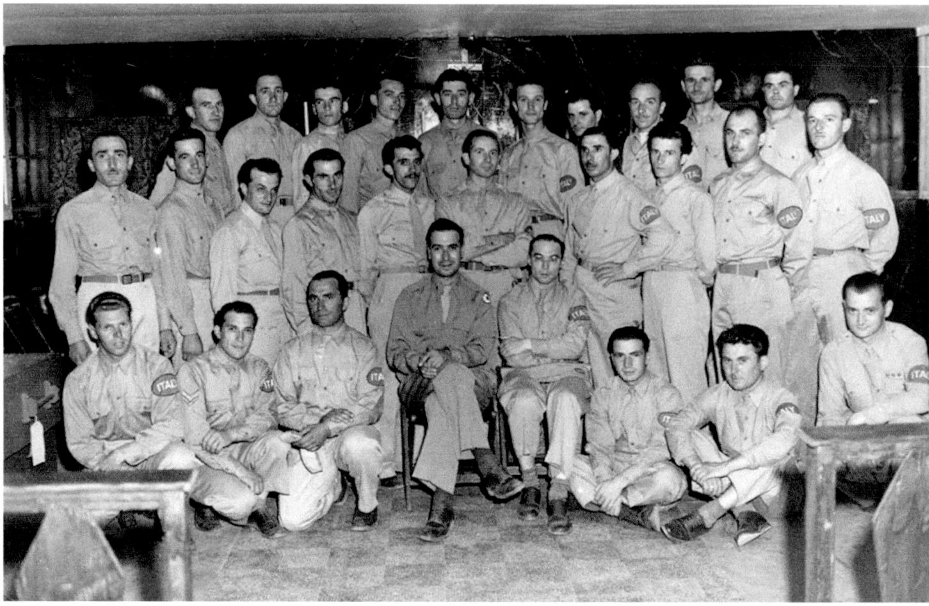

ISU at Utah ASF with Father Raphael Monteleone (Italian born US Army Chaplain), courtesy of Andrea Selmi.

Escapes were expected and did occur at several locations. Most of them were short in duration and distance, usually ending with an easy capture or surrender since the object was only able to get outside the fence for a while. Some were more serious, with bigger plans and groups of men, also usually ending in surrender. Just a couple of men were able to remain at large until many years after the war ended. No reports of sabotage or terrorism were ever associated with these escapes.

One of the Italian groups had been moved from Italy to Africa to Lordsburg, NM, to Ogden, UT, accompanied by a big brown dog.

POW work included occupations required for the maintenance of the camps, such as cooking, cleaning, clothing and shoe repairs, landscaping, etc.

They also were hired out for canning and farming in the community, including pruning orchards and planting as well as harvesting. They also worked on dams, railroads, orchards, mining, quarrying, and forestry. The businesses and farmers paid the government a minimum wage and the POWs were paid 80 cents a day, comparable to the wage for a civilian day laborer.

Even the Ogden Chamber of Commerce hired POWs. And Italian POWs at Fort Monmouth, NJ, were making violins.

Other POWs were working on occupations labeled military, such as at hospitals, supply offices, post exchanges, construction, dying uniforms, landscaping, and woodworking.

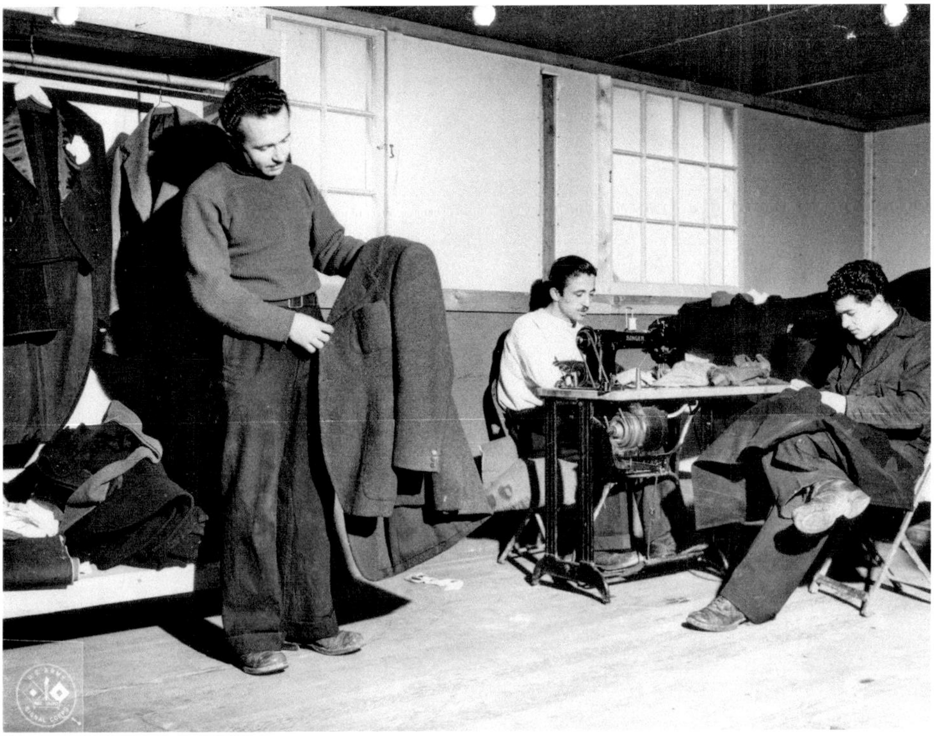

Italian tailors at Utah ASF Depot, courtesy of Special Collections Department, Stewart Library, Weber State University.

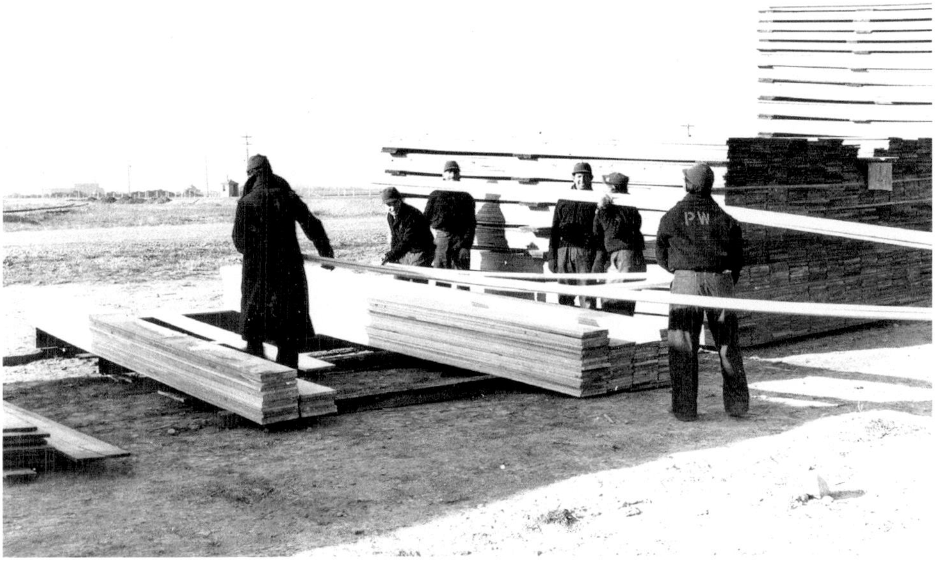

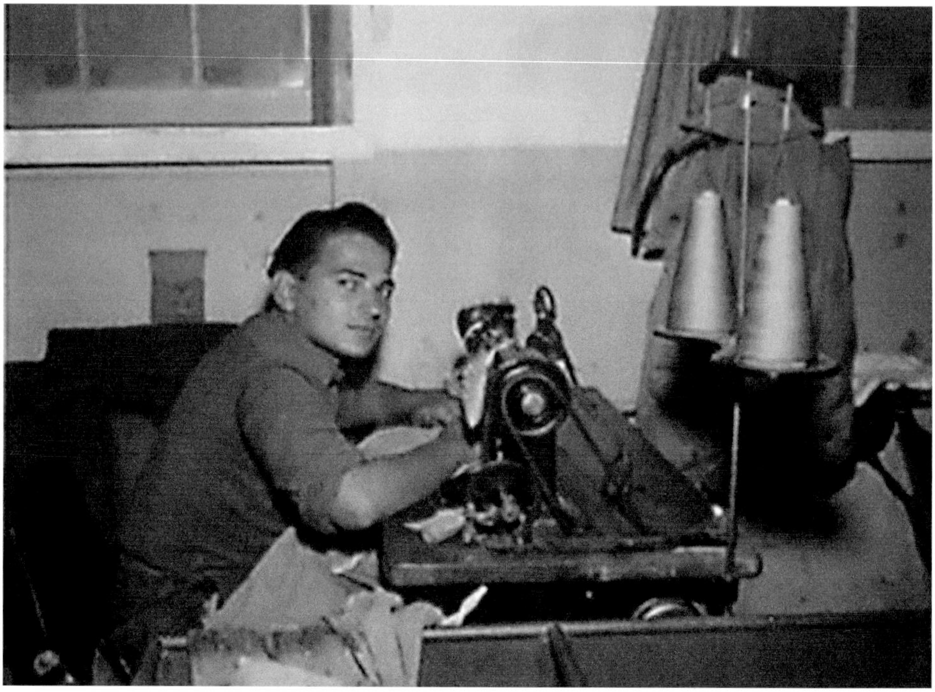

German and Italian POW tailors at Utah ASF Depot. Courtesy of Special Collections Department, Stewart Library, Weber State University.

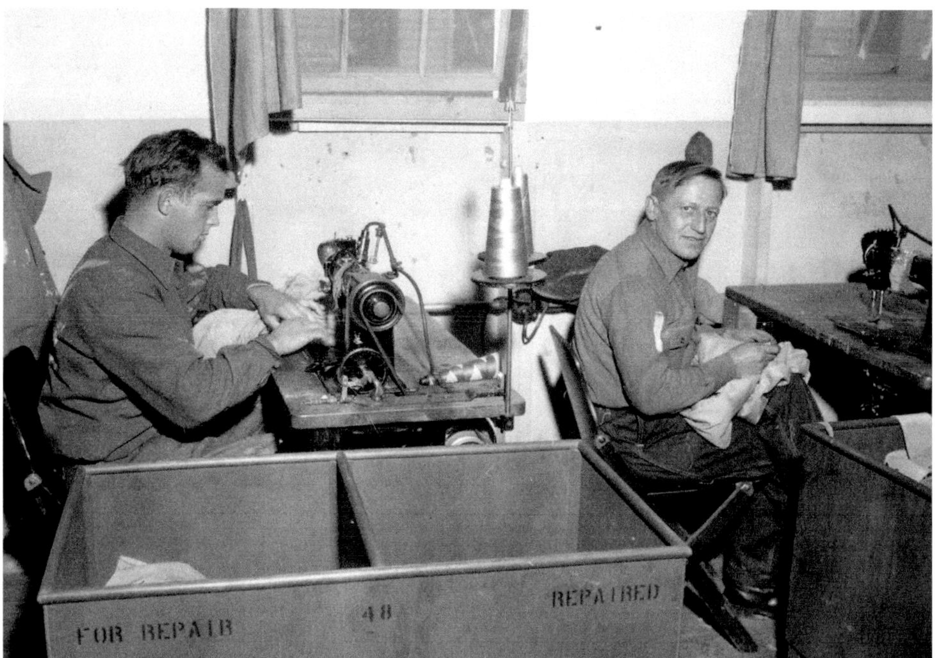

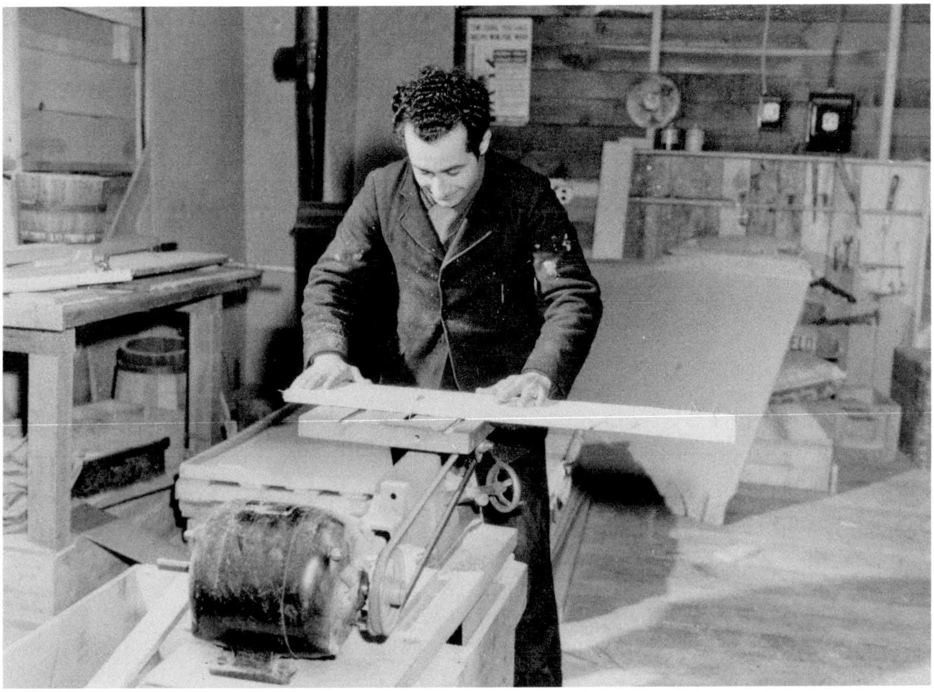

Above: Italian in Carpentry shop at Utah ASF Depot, courtesy of Special Collections Department, Stewart Library, Weber State University.

Right: German POW railroad workers, courtesy of Special Collections Department, Stewart Library, Weber State University.

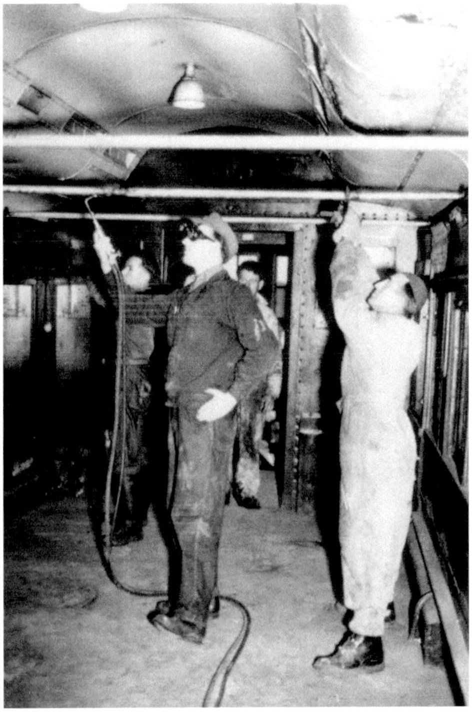

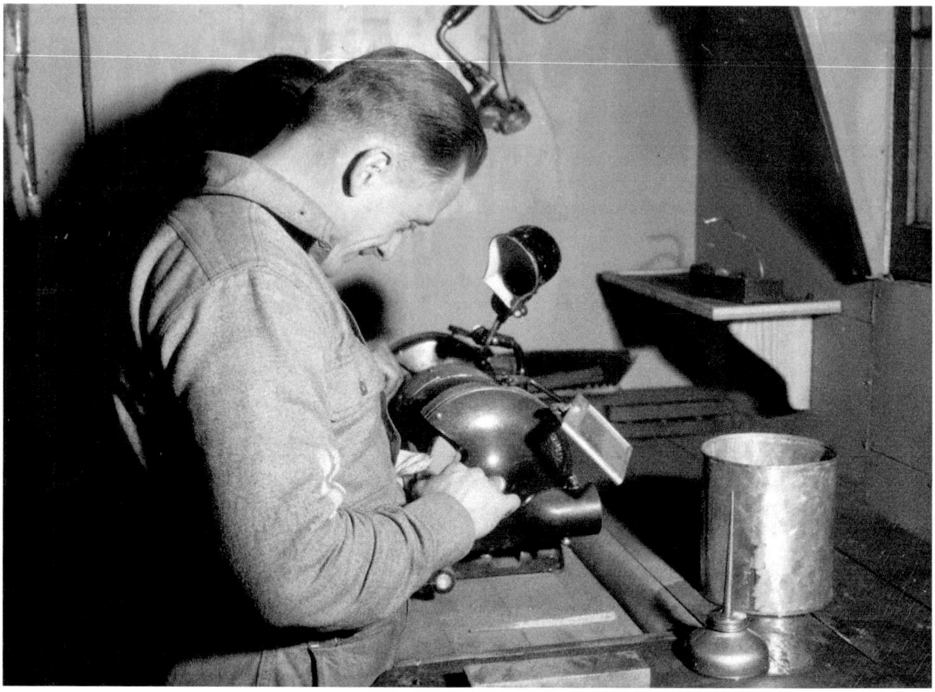

German POWs at Ogden Depot, courtesy of Special Collections Department, Stewart Library, Weber State University.

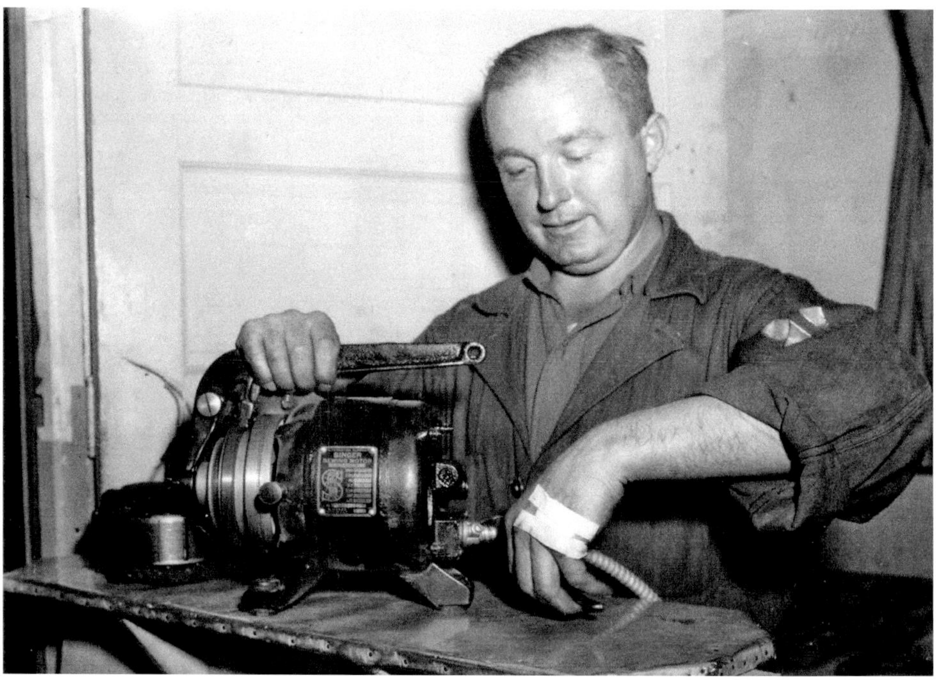

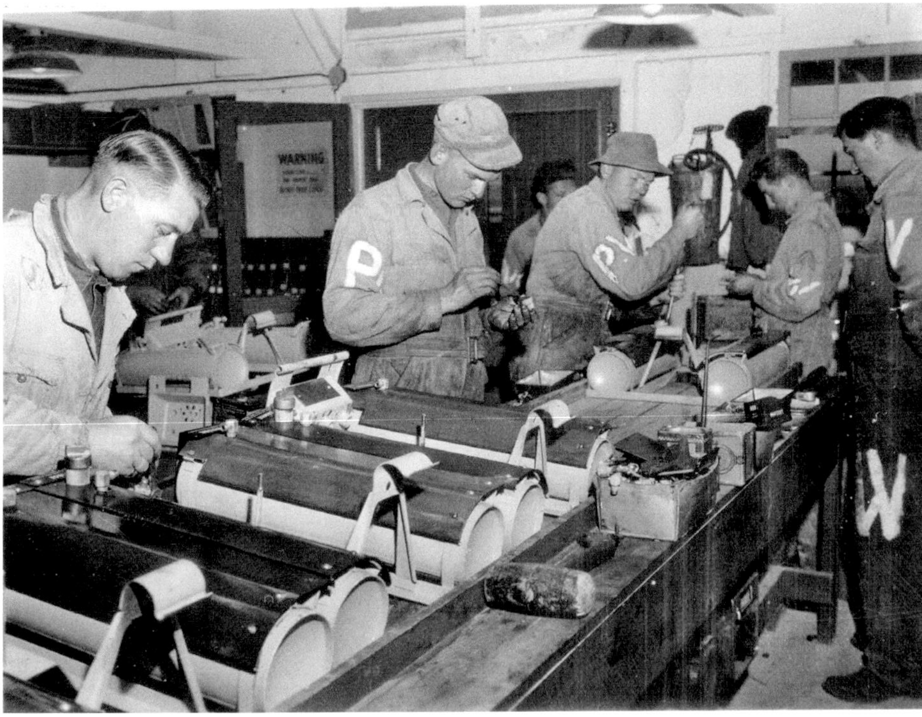

German POWs at Ogden Depot, courtesy of Special Collections Department, Stewart Library, Weber State University.

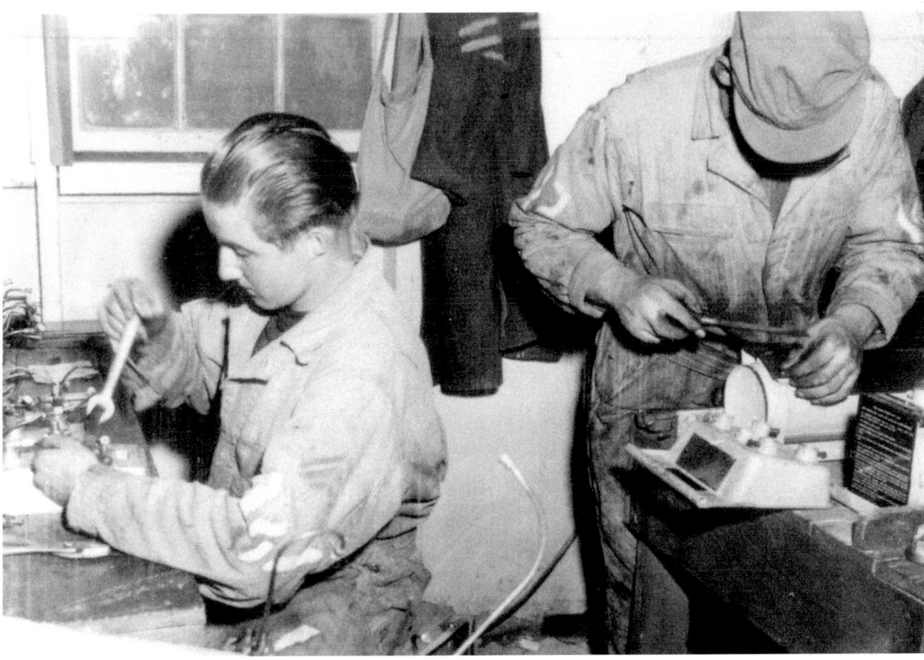

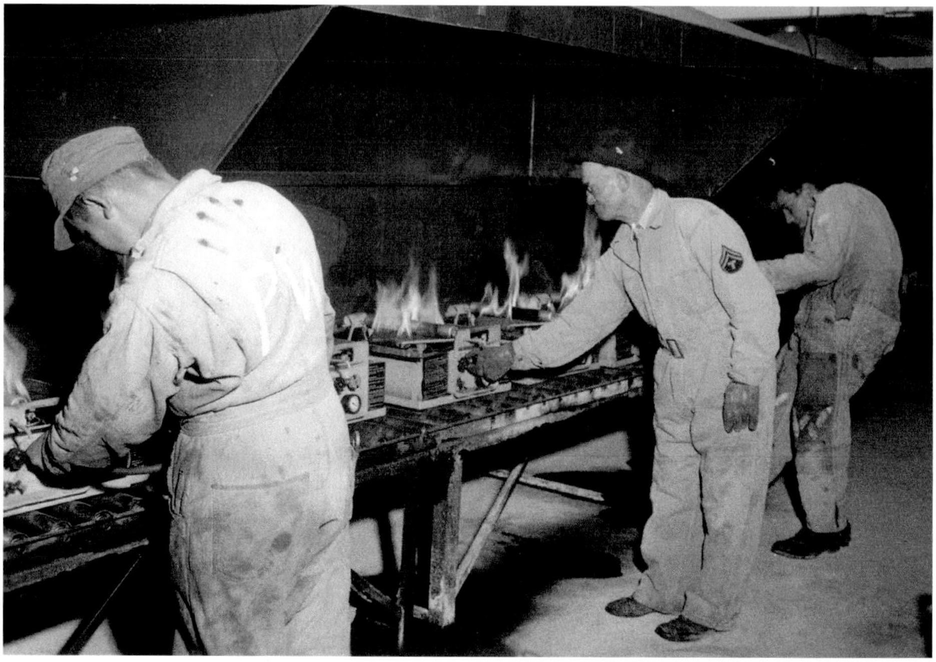

German (above) and Italian (below) POWs at Ogden Depot, courtesy of Special Collections Department, Stewart Library, Weber State University.

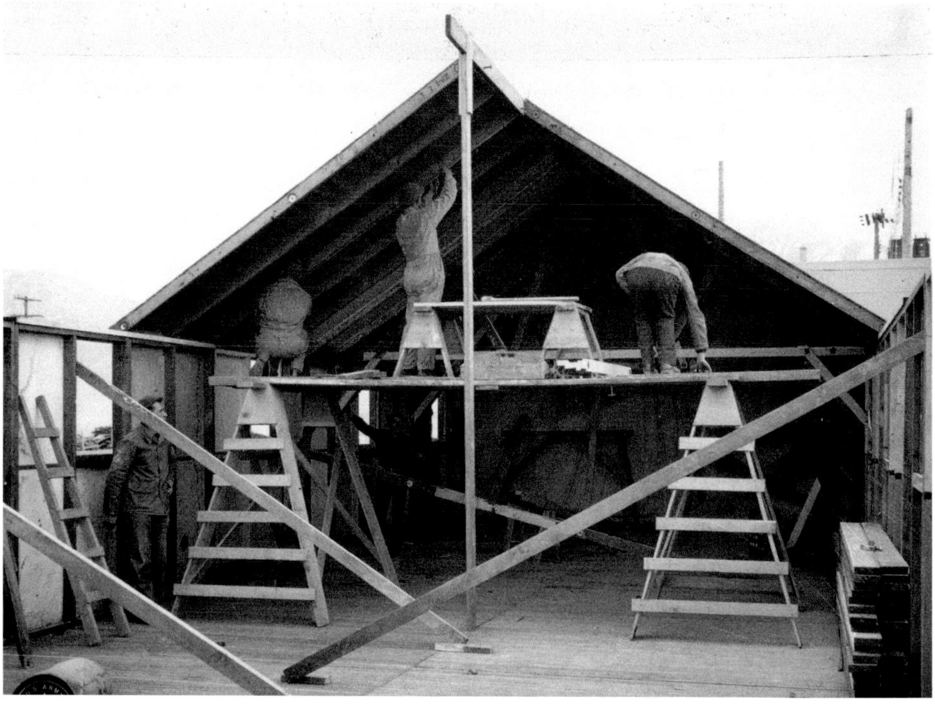

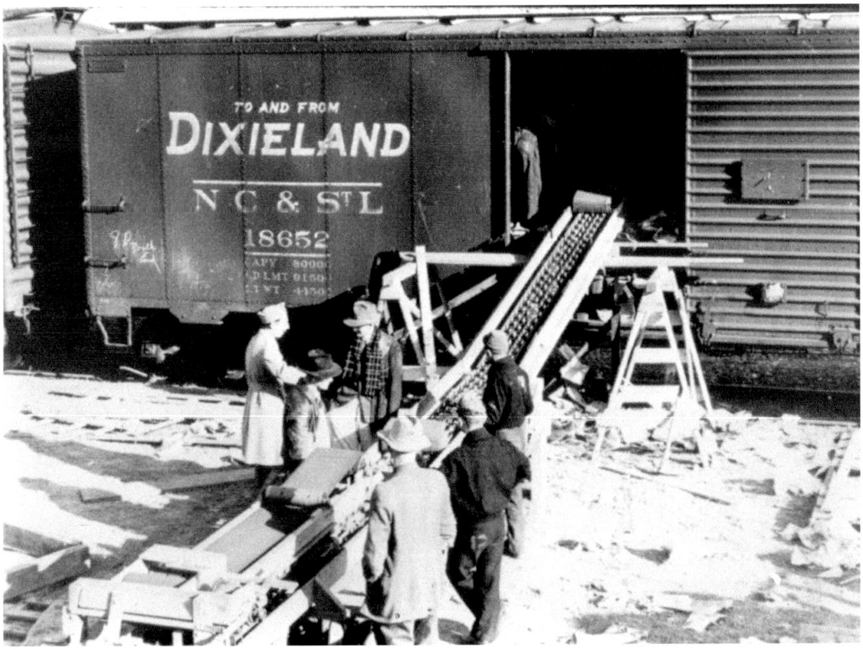

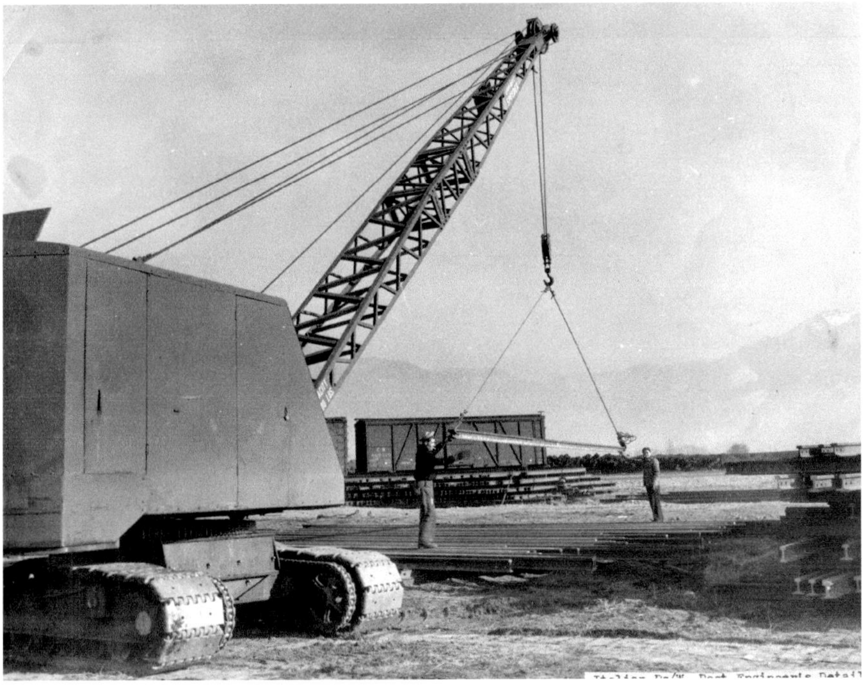

Italian POWs at Ogden Depot, courtesy of Special Collections Department, Stewart Library, Weber State University.

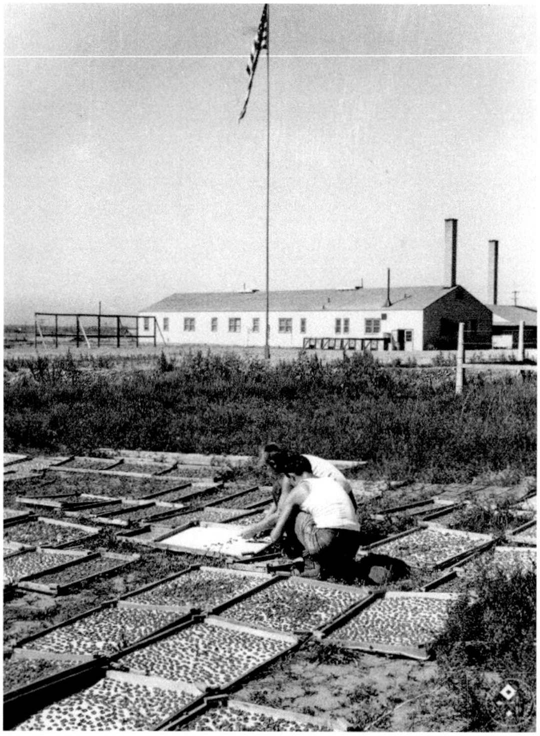

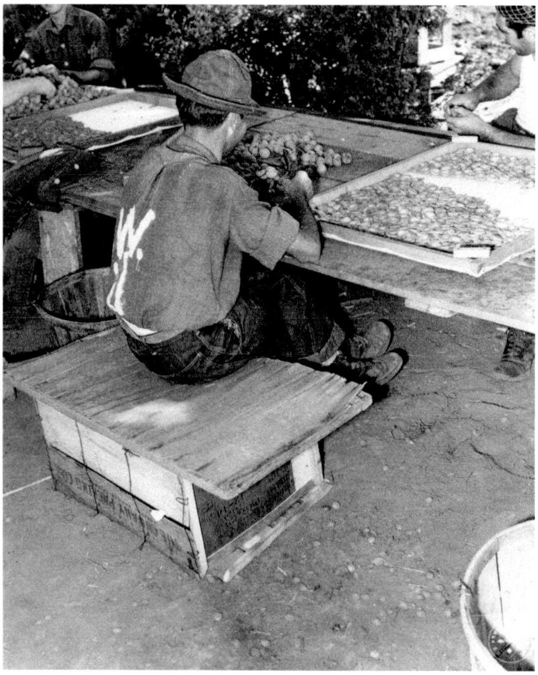

Italian POWs at Ogden Depot, courtesy of Special Collections Department, Stewart Library, Weber State University.

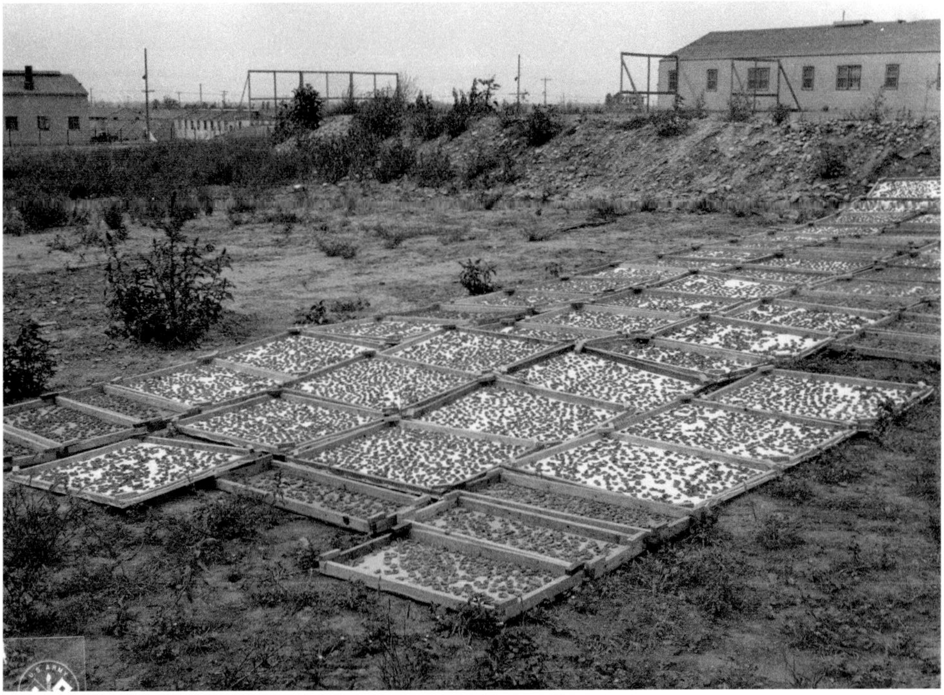

Italian POWs at Ogden Depot, courtesy of Special Collections Department, Stewart Library, Weber State University.

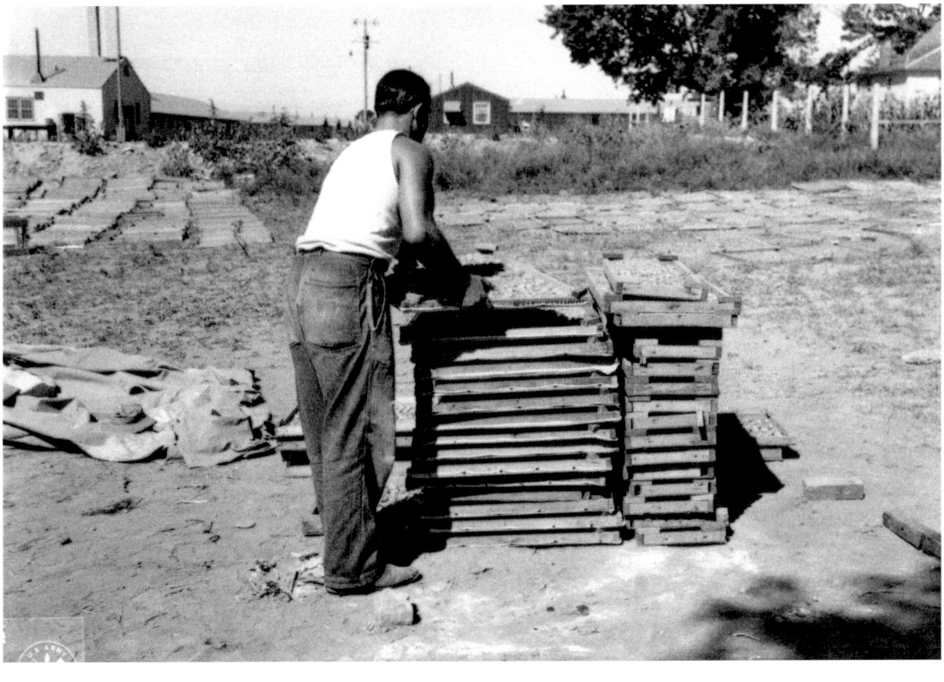

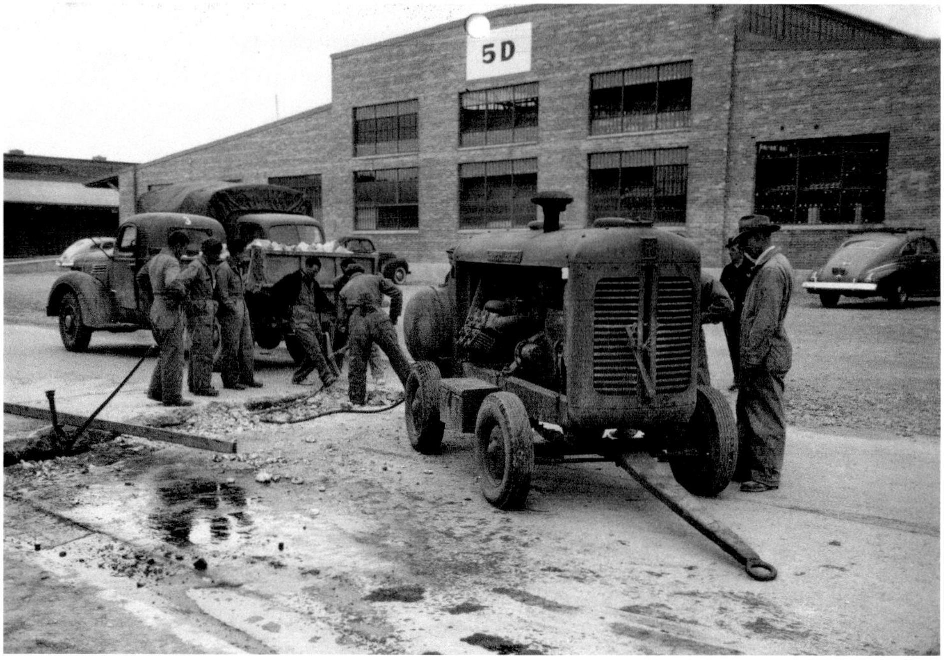

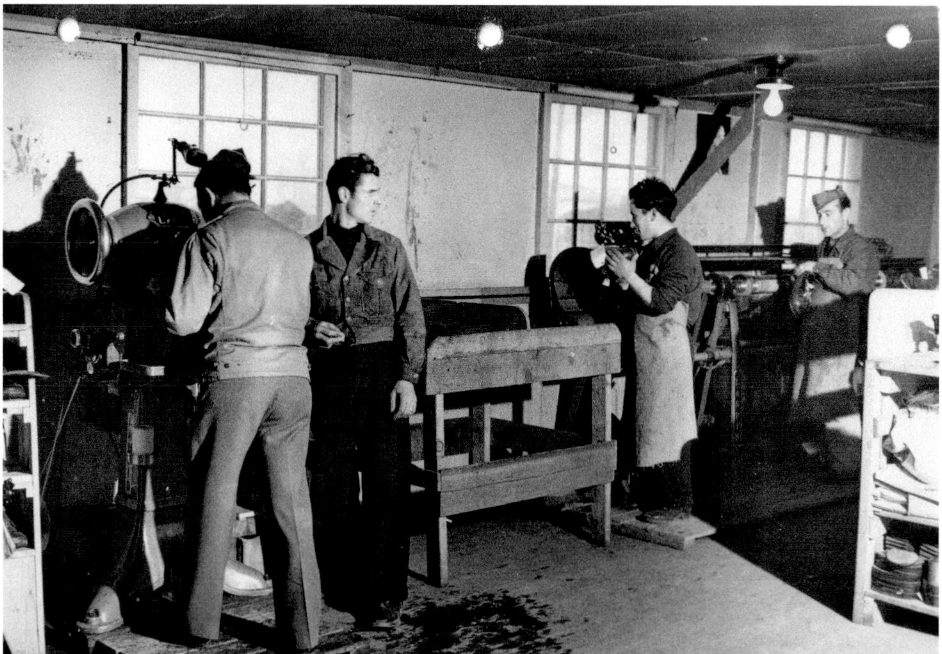

Italian POWs at Ogden Depot, courtesy of Special Collections Department, Stewart Library, Weber State University.

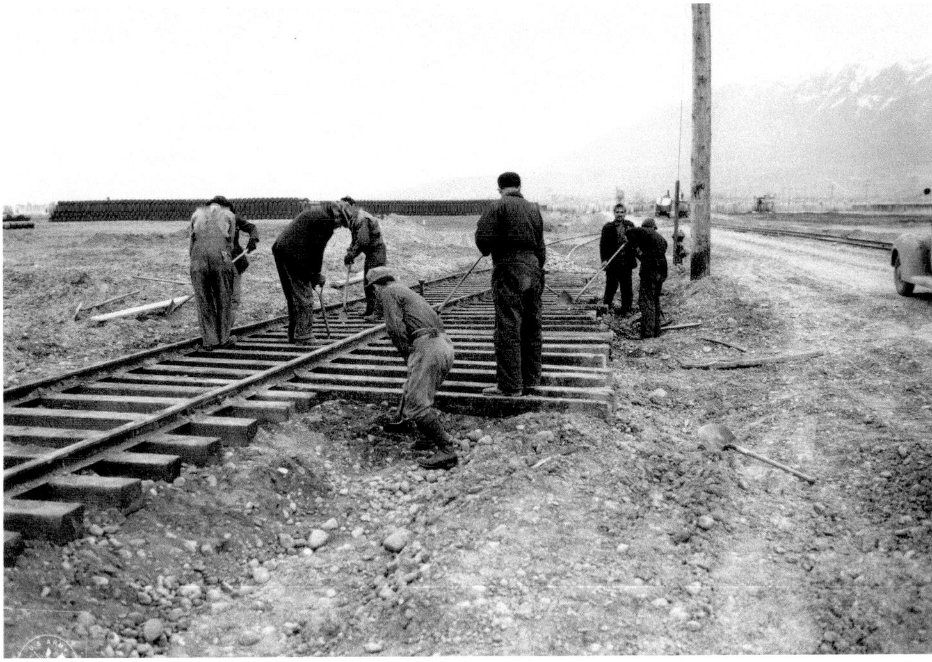

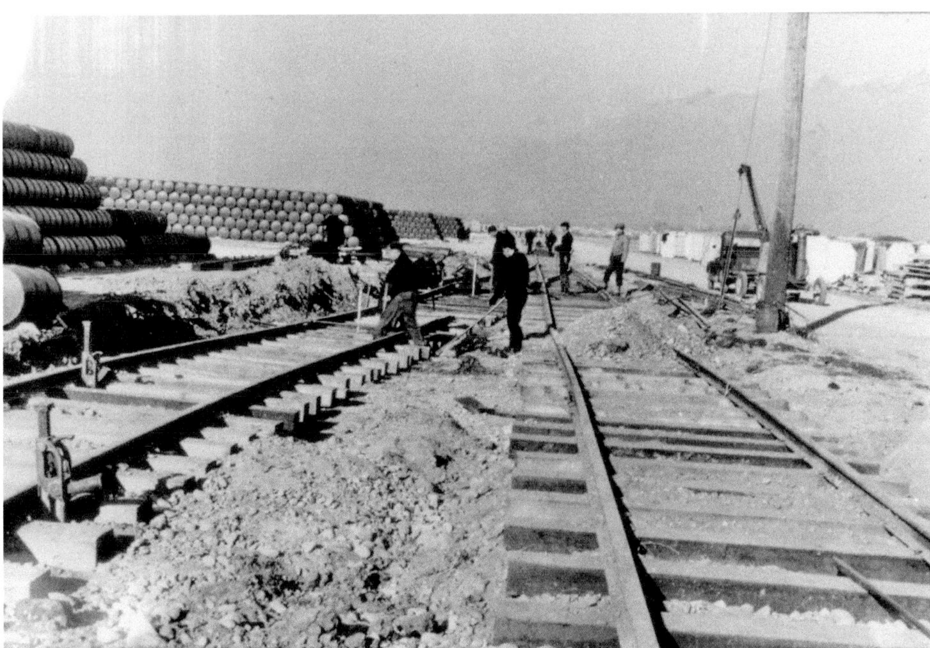

Italian POWs at Ogden Depot, courtesy of Special Collections Department, Stewart Library, Weber State University.

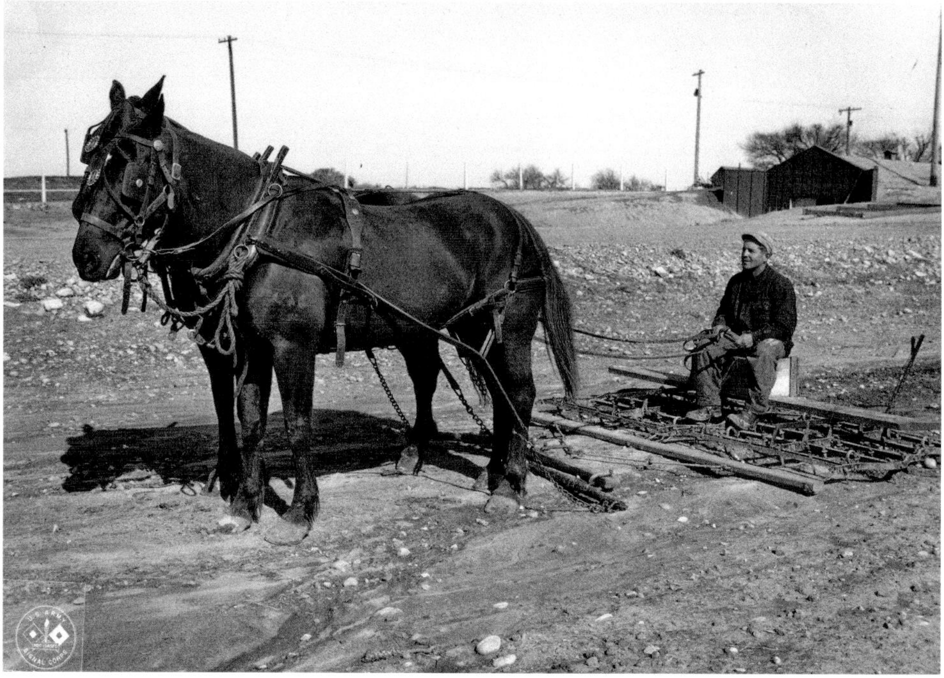

Italian POW farmers at Utah ASF Depot, courtesy of Special Collections Department, Stewart Library, Weber State University.

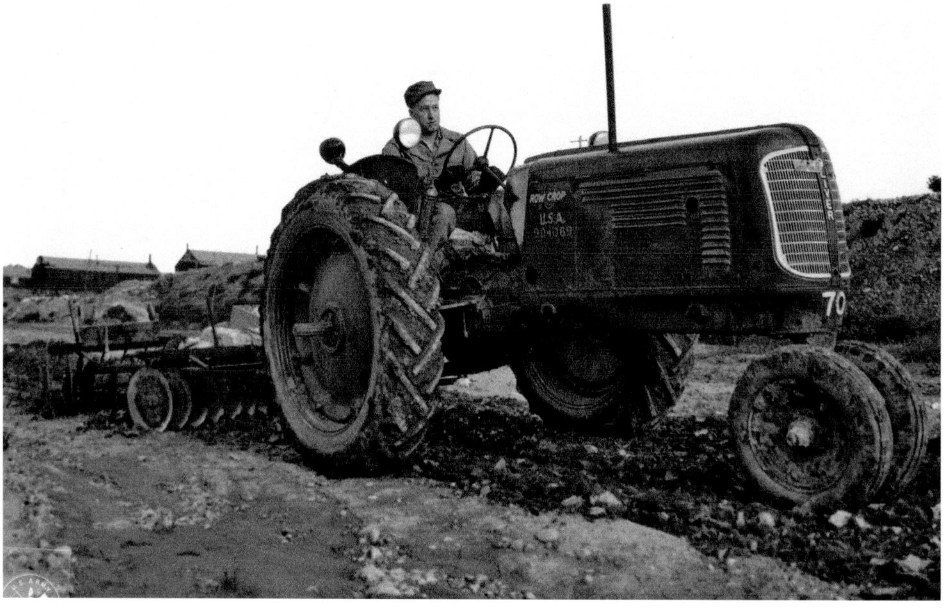

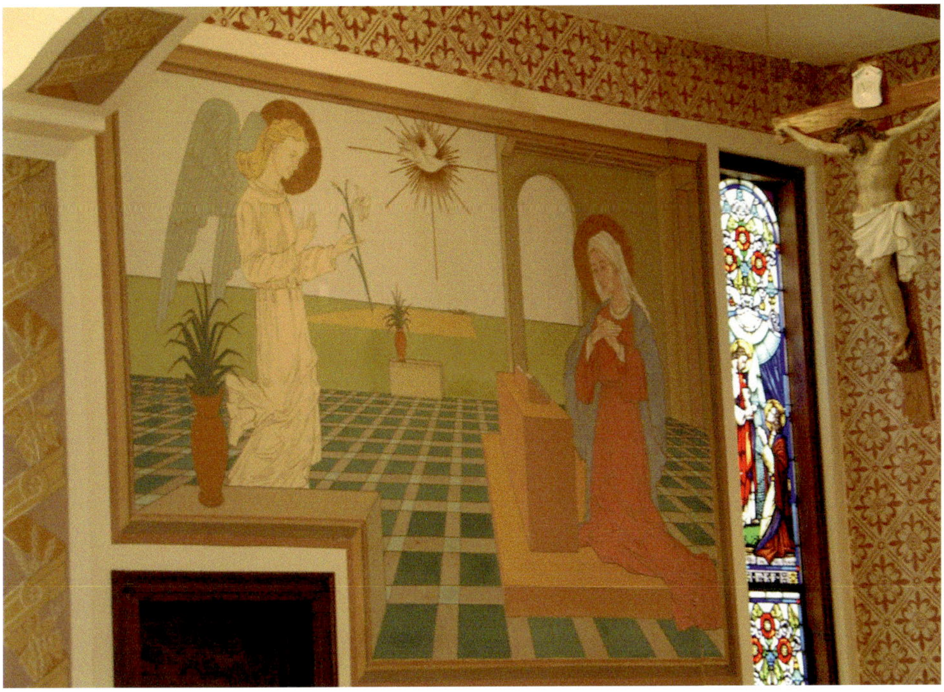

Sometimes POWs worked on community service projects outside the camp. The Catholic Church of St. Mary's in Umbarger, TX, was beautifully decorated with murals and other artwork by Italian POWs from nearby Camp Hereford. Courtesy of John Saffell.

The POWs were paid at a rate of $3.00 per month if they did work (enlisted) or $24 a month for officers who weren't allowed to work. Those who did work were paid $.80 to $1.20/day depending on if working for local farmers or private companies. This was paid to them in coupons they could use at the canteen, although ISU members could receive 1/3 of their pay in cash to use in town. An office of the Italian Army which made sure all the former POWs received their due pay was opened at the end of the war and continued until very recently. I worked in their offices in 2004 and was able to obtain records of transfers from camp to camp and the health record for a POW (with authorization from his son). Geneva Convention required that officers be separated. In April 1944, 160 Italian officers (Lt. Col. down to Major) arrived at Utah ASF from Wangsgard, MO. When German enlisted men arrived to take the place of the Italian POWs who had not joined the ISU, those officers were moved to Camp Rupert.

Italian Service Units

The fall of Mussolini and resultant change in that government's position in the war from Axis to Allied required some changes regarding Italian POWs. It was quickly determined that releasing them would not be the best solution. The original idea of Italian POWs being organized into units to provide labor similar to the Civilian Conservation Corps (CCC) was first proposed by the U.S. Secretary of War in October 1943. This would require separation of fascist Italian POWs from those willing to work for the war effort as co-belligerents.

They would be "attached to and placed under the command of the U.S. Army ... Therefore, the plan included these features: (1) Italian prisoners would be organized into numbered Italian service companies consisting of 5 officers and 177 enlisted men ... (4) An Italian service unit headquarters would be established under ASF and would be commanded by an American officer ... The new plan provided for Italian Service Units (ISUs) to be organized from volunteer Italian PW officers, non-commissioned officers, and enlisted men under approved tables of organization and equipment, less weapons. Initially, two U.S. Army officers and ten enlisted men were to be attached to each unit for supervision; but these were to be reduced, consistent with efficiency and security, to a minimum of one officer and five enlisted men."

The ranking Italian General over the new ISU on 26 January 1944, Claudio Trezzani, states, "The units should be commanded by Italian officers, in this proportion; one first or second lieutenant for 30 to 35 enlisted men (platoon), one captain for 4 platoons (company), one senior officer for 3 companies (battalion), one colonel for 3 battalions (regiment)." That letter is followed in the Italian Army file at Stato Maggiore Esercito in Rome by an apparent American response with no name or date attached stating, "It is contemplated organizing Italian Service Units according to American tables of organization with Italian military personnel in all authorized positions, American officers and enlisted men in the smallest possible numbers will be attached as custodians, for liaison, to issue operational directives, sign payrolls and charges, and have general responsibility for the units to higher American authority." Italian Generals Frattini and De Simone were moved to ISU headquarters at Fort Wadsworth from Camp Monticello.

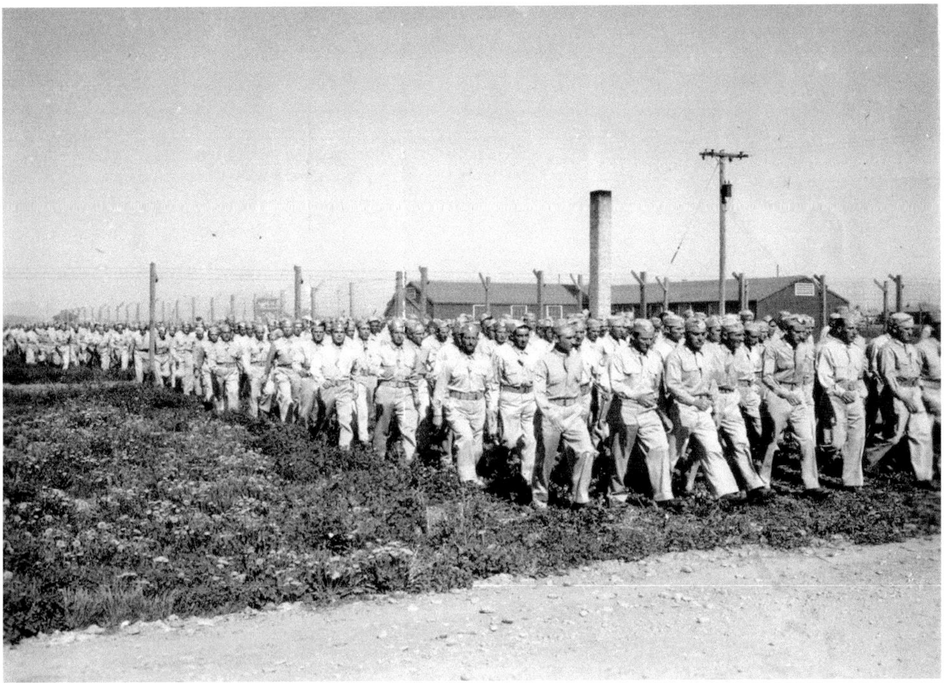

Italian Service Units at Utah ASF Depot, courtesy of Special Collections Department, Stewart Library, Weber State University.

The ISU program was under the command of Brig. General J. M. Eager, from the PMGO. The ASF retained the responsibilities of plans, policies and procedures as well as the designation and strength of units and training programs and doctrines. Each unit had American personnel of one officer and five enlisted men at a minimum. Service commands were responsible for all other ISU functions and activities. Interviews with former translators assigned to those units confirmed that one American NCO was a translator for the unit.

The ISU had increased responsibilities resulting in increased privileges for the 65% of Italian POWs who signed up to serve in Italian Service Units. The new units were activated progressively with 600 POWs organized in the first week of March 1944, 1,000 for the first two weeks of April, 3,000 the third week in April, and 4,000 each succeeding week until completed. While a letter was sent to the camps from Badoglio in Rome, it was vague and general and the Italian King never spoke (wrote) on the subject. This left many men in confusion as to the best course of action. Their families were in German-occupied Italy and many feared repercussions for such a visible support of their former enemy. The screening from ISU to POW and reverse was continuous to ensure that only the most cooperative POWs were allowed the privileges of the ISU.

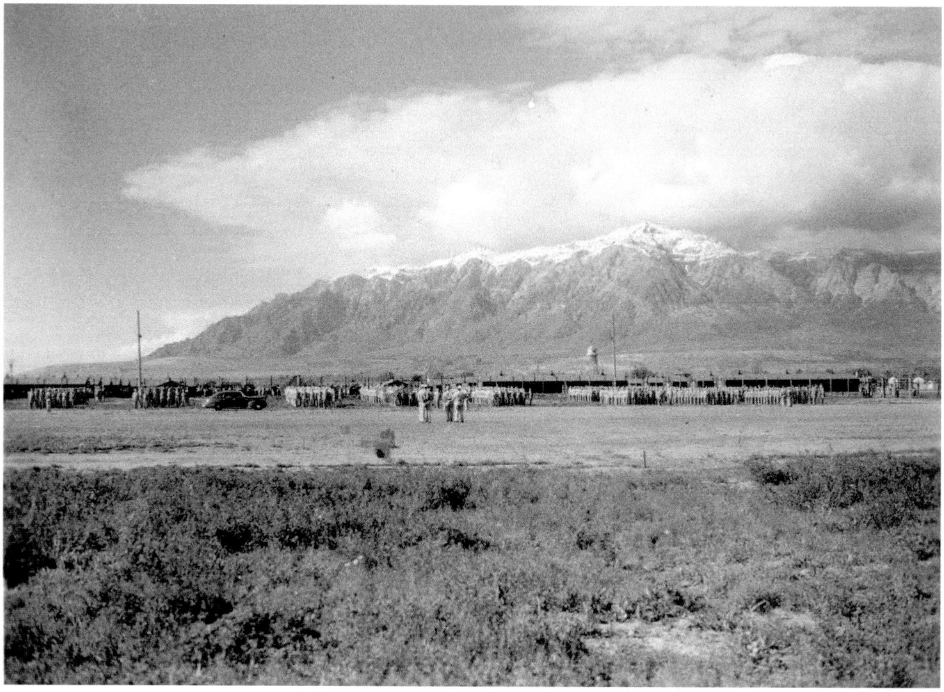

Courtesy of Special Collections Department, Stewart Library, Weber State University.

At Utah ASF Depot in Ogden, those men who signed the agreement to join the ISU remained to work. Those who didn't were sent to Camp Rupert (Idaho) or Tulare Lake (California), according to the Utah ASF historian. But further research shows that Rupert was a temporary location since they don't appear on population reports for that location kept by the PMGO.

ISU units were held in separate camps from Italian POWs. Those POWs who didn't join the ISU were classified as fascist. Instruction in English stressed in these new units, while the same housing and wages applied, with the addition of ten cents a day for a gratuitous allowance. Two thirds of the wage was paid in coupons and one third in cash. Rules against fraternization between members of ISU and American military did not apply. ISU Service Clubs were created to give them greater access to reading materials and a quiet place to relax since they did not have access to the U.S. Army clubs. Dances and other special events were organized through the ISU Service Clubs.

Training programs for ISU was the same as for American personnel on similar jobs, less tactics and weapons training.

Work restrictions imposed by Geneva Convention were lifted with the consent of the Badoglio government of Italy, except for combat, work at ports of embarkation within

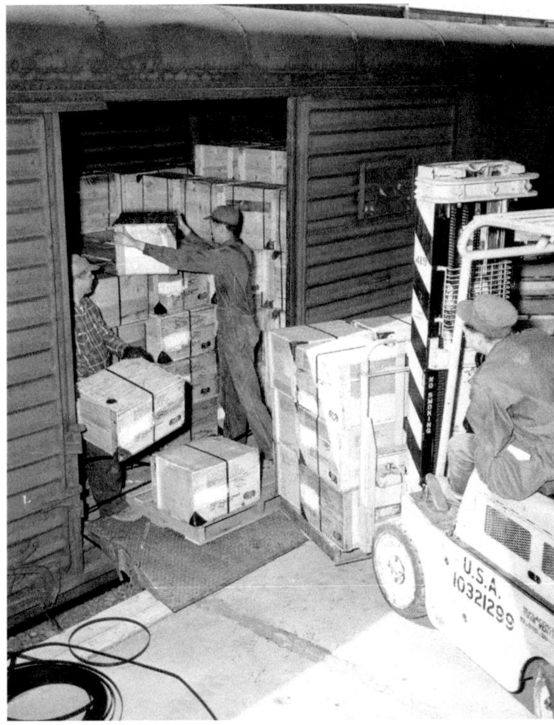

Loading supplies at Utah ASF Depot, courtesy of Special Collections Department, Stewart Library, Weber State University.

continental U.S., and work with explosives. Their efforts released U.S. personnel for overseas duties and helped to bring about the successful conclusion of the war.

ISU units began to ship to the European Theater to assist with support and supply from Africa and into Italy as part of the liberation of Italy in the following theaters of operation: North African, Eastern European, Mediterranean. Apparently, some of these units were moved overseas at the discretion of the ISU command and the PMGO was not informed.

Mail restrictions were reduced to the same standards as American personnel for domestic correspondence. Regulations were the same as POWs for international mail. The new ISU Uniforms were the same khaki as U.S. uniforms, with a patch (Italy) on the left shoulder. At least one man was court-martialed for removing the Italian patch on a night out on the town, leading to accusations of being AWOL. However, he was simply reprimanded instead of sent to a POW camp.

The POWs and their employers and guards weren't supposed to fraternize. But, of course they did. While some of the initial contact was antagonistic, many friendships and romances resulted.

ISU men were permitted weekend passes when signed out by a sponsor. Many Italian communities utilized these privileges to give some of the ISU men a family gathering, social activity, or dance. Some of the dances at the ISU Service Club included invitations to young women in the community.

Additionally, ISU members were given day passes into town for movies, dances, and just sightseeing. In Ogden, buses were used to transport ISU men from their barracks to St. Joseph's Catholic church in downtown Ogden for dances. These dances were organized so that one night a week was for officers and three nights a week for enlisted men. Decorating was done by the ISU and they provided the orchestra on Thursday nights. The jukebox and games were provided by Catholic groups in Ogden and Salt Lake City. Of course, the greatest attraction was meeting and dancing with American girls.

Some of these meetings resulted in marriages. The POWs couldn't marry, but once engaged, and returned (by June 1946), the troop transports bringing GIs home were taking these women with their escorts to Italy with the proper paperwork to marry so they could return to the U.S. with their new husbands. Five of these couples settled in Ogden, UT.

Some of these meetings had unhappy endings. The local culture was against marrying a man of a different ethnic or religious background, plus some families feared that their girls would follow the men to Italy and never return. So those romances were discouraged, even after they created children. Some of those children were adopted out, while some stayed with their mothers who married other men here in the U.S. after the war. Some

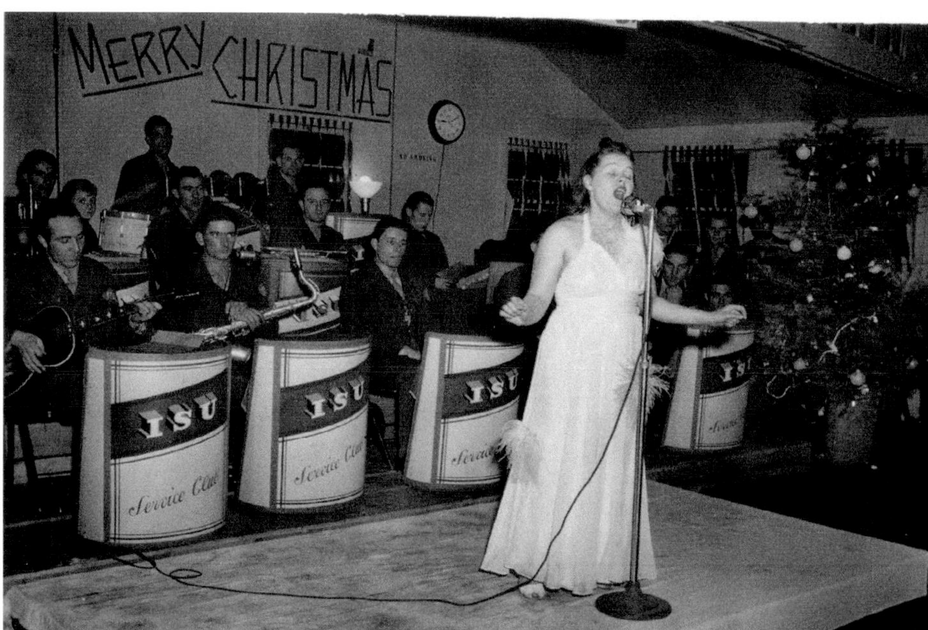

ISU party at Utah ASF Depot, courtesy of Special Collections Department, Stewart Library, Weber State University.

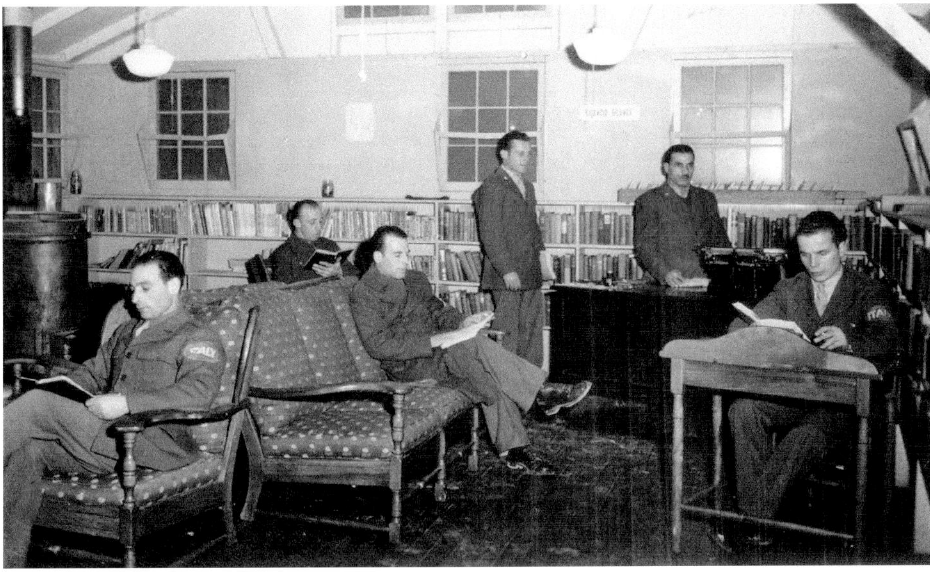

Italian Service Club at Utah ASF Depot, courtesy of Special Collections Department, Stewart Library, Weber State University.

of those children sought their Italian families all their lives. Fortunately, we have assisted with some happy reunions.

Public opinion varied as shown in a variety of newspapers from those years. There were some escapes, usually associated with meeting a girl outside the camp for reasons that had nothing to do with national security.

The Italian POWs held a unique position as both POWs and Allies that created different experiences for them than for their German counterparts. In Utah and other ISU locations, these differences meant more opportunities to not only work with the residents, but also to socialize with them. The resulting friendships (and some marriages) show the very positive results of their experiences under very difficult circumstances.

Death in the Camps

A total of 1,074 burials, including 880 Germans (includes three Russians, four Austrians, one Yugoslavian, one Czech and one Turk), 172 Italians, 23 Japanese (includes one Korean) out of 1,076 POWs who died while held in the U.S. during World War II.

Many of the larger camps had their own cemeteries. After the war, the cemeteries from those camps which had been closed and some other locations, were moved to National Cemeteries to provide the perpetual care demanded by the Geneva Convention.

While most of the headstones were standard issue for U.S. military, there are some exceptions. At Fort Douglas, Eilert's stone was put up by the POWs with the permission of the camp commander and paid for by the POWs.

The funeral services were often accompanied by Americans as well as POWs, sometimes also a POW choir and/or band and a symbolic series of shots fired by a military guard.

Rumors insist that most of the POWs who died here were shipped home. The truth is that the U.S. government was willing to ship them, if the family bore the cost. Of course, most of the families were simply unable to bear that burden at the end of a war they lost. Only one Italian, Renato Facchini, was returned to Italy before February 1947, while Francesco Erriquez was returned to Italy in 2011. Apparently, none of the Germans were returned since the names in the original reports match the current cemetery records.

Some of the deaths were accidents in the course of work or recreation. Others were later deemed murders by Nazi extremists. Some were suicides, particularly at the end of the war.

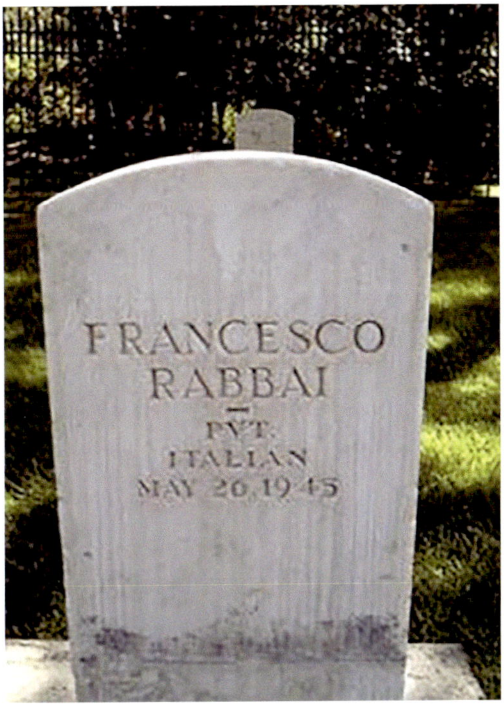

Above: Fort Douglas, UT, photo by author.

Right: Fort Douglas Cemetery, photo by author.

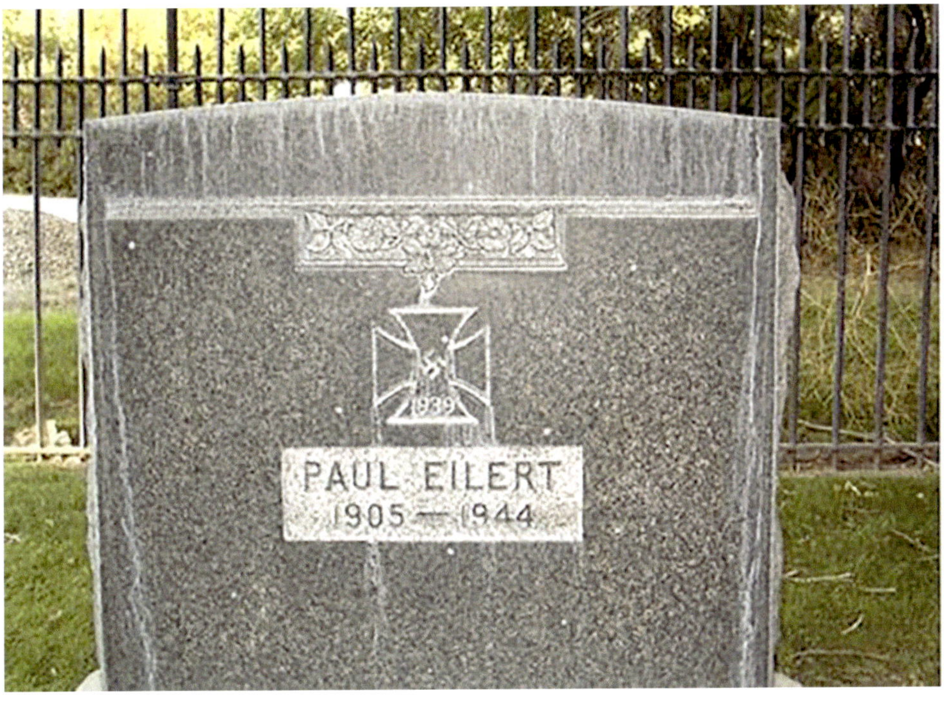

Returning Home (1945-46)

Certain camps were designated as separation centers (like Florence, AZ) and the POWs were moved through them, then on to ports of embarkation on both coasts for the trip home. The first returned were the Italian officers as co-belligerents. The next group was the ISU members, then the rest.

The Geneva Convention of 1929 required that POWs be returned home at the end of a war. However, the large numbers provided some logistics problems. Generally, troop ships bringing U.S. troops home turned around full of POWs. However, treaties with all countries provided that some of the POWs (not ISU) were returned to France, the U.S.S.R. and Great Britain to assist with reconstruction efforts. Some of the men in Great Britain and France worked there as long as four years before returning home. The U.S.S.R. finally released the surviving prisoners ten years later.

Warnings were made regarding German POWs scheduled to be returned to the U.S.S.R. It was only after the first group was killed on the dock by the crew of the Soviet vessel which met them that other arrangements were made for those men.

Some POWs claimed status as U.S. citizens and requested permission to stay, but were returned to avoid the legal complications.

Some locations requested that their POWs stay long enough to complete the fall harvest and that was permitted when it could be arranged. The last POWs were repatriated (out of the U.S.) by 30 June 1946, except 141 Germans, 20 Italians, and one Japanese serving sentences in U.S. penal institutions, plus the two Germans who revealed themselves many years later.

A large number of ports were utilized as departure points for the returning POWs. They included:

Los Angeles, CA
Charleston, SC
New Orleans, LA
Hampton Roads, VA
New York, NY

Boston, MA
San Francisco, CA
Seattle, WA
Halifax, Nova Scotia

Those same troop vessels were used to transport American fiancés of POWs to Naples and Genoa. These American war brides often spent a few months in Italy to complete the red tape required for a marriage there and assisting their new families in rebuilding. They then brought their husbands home to America. These stories were shared by Pat and Maria Pisani and by Beth Giordana, war brides and American girls who made the trip to Italy to marry their former POW husbands.

Part of the logistics meant that after the U.S. troops returned home, their European war brides and families were shipped home on the same troop ships, slightly modified to accommodate families with small children. The Cary Grant movie, *I Was a Male War Bride*, is more funny than factual, but it is based on the real transport of war brides from Europe to America.

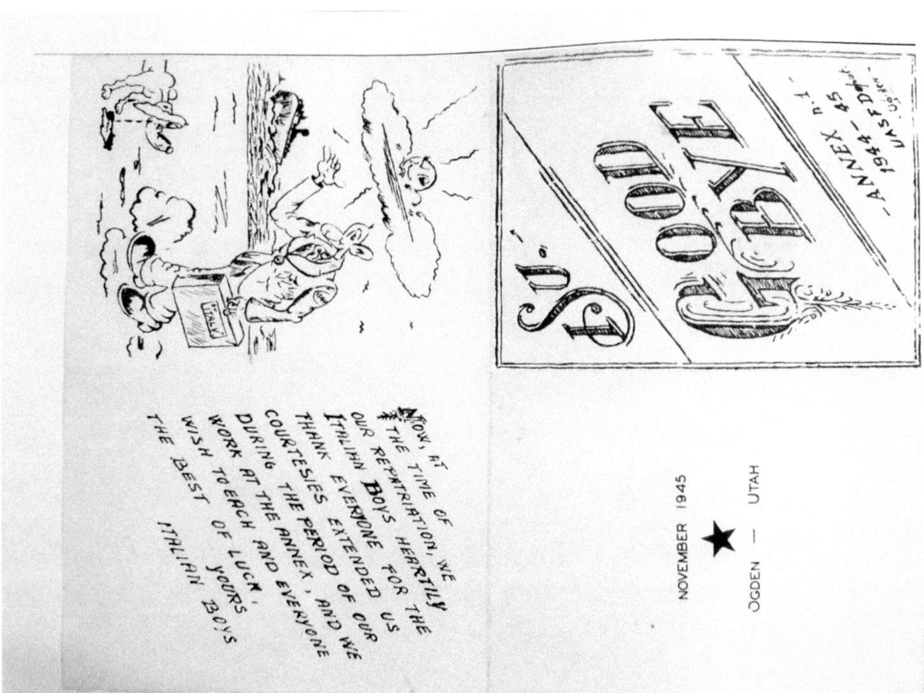

This goodbye note from the Italian Boys at Ogden Depot was saved by Mario Saggese, one of those boys, and used here courtesy of his daughter, living in the United States.

Other former POWs made the move to live in the U.S. from ten to twenty years later. They settled in areas where they had worked as POWs, apparently in nearly every location in the country. Only local newspapers have these stories, so it's hard to get statistics. I recently found an article, "Returning to America: German Prisoners of War and the American Experience" by Barbara Schmitter Heisler (details in the bibliography).

The trip to marry in Italy was made by a young woman from Louisville, KY, who had met her husband when he was a prisoner at Camp Atterbury, Indiana. They'd met at a dance sponsored by the local Italian-American community for the Italian POWs. I met this lovely woman at a POW Reunion at Camp Atterbury in 2010 along with her children. They were regular attendees at this annual event and had wonderful stories to share. They also have a display at the Camp Atterbury Museum, across the road from the main gate to Camp Atterbury, now a Reserve Military Training Facility.

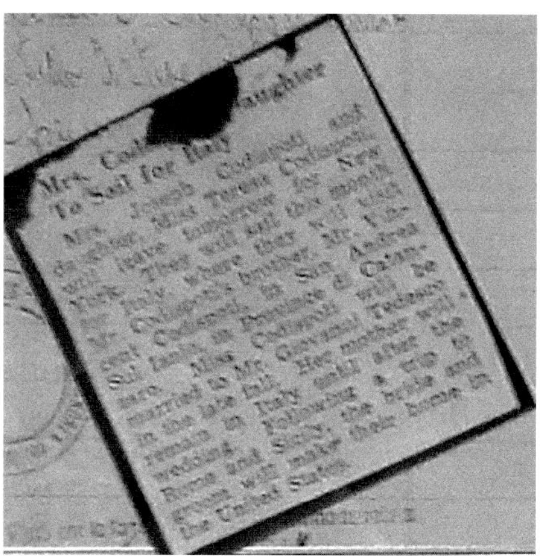

Museum display, Camp Atterbury, photo by author.

After the War

Some of the camps were determined to be surplus, so the property was auctioned off and the land was sold or transferred to another federal or state agency. This was a thorough process, leaving behind very little in the way of buildings to mark the former camps today.

The POW personnel records were returned to other nations in whose military they served in 1955.

The German records are now available at:
Deutsche Dienstelle (WASt)
Postfach 51 06 57
D-13400 Berlin
Germany

The Italian records are now available at:
Ministero della Difesa
via Mattia Battistini, 113, 7 Piano
00167 Roma
Italy

The Japanese records are now available at:
Military History Department National Institute for Defense Studies
2-2-1 Nakameguro, Meguro-ku
Tokyo, 153-8648
Japan

The former POWs held in the U.S. mostly held good memories of their time here. Some returned to become U.S. citizens, like Ernst Bulkat who lived in Orem, UT. Information on them can usually be found in local papers in the 1970s and 1980s when local news groups interviewed them in a resurgence of interest in the history of the area during WWII.

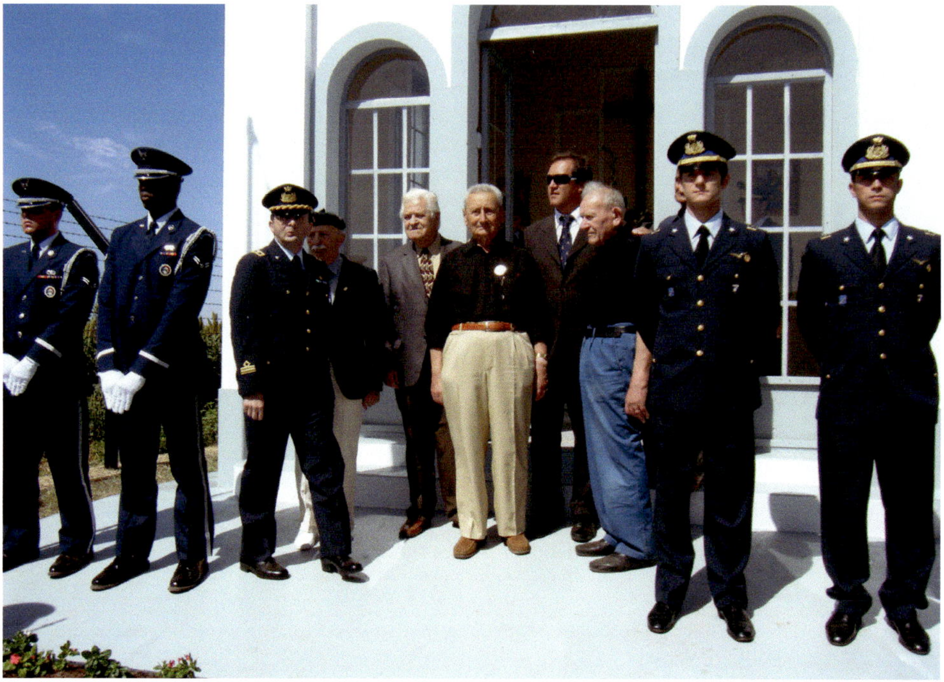

This photo was taken at the 2009 reunion at Camp Hereford, TX. The U.S. Army is on the left, the former POWs center, and the Italian Air Force on the right. Photo by John Saffell of these men in front of the chapel built by Italian POWs.

Some former POWs returned as tourists to show their families where they'd spent part of the war. Some groups held reunions of groups of POWs who had been at a particular location to facilitate their return there with some ceremony and lots of memories.

Some diaries and recollections have been published by former POWs. See Heino R. Erichsen's *The Reluctant Warrior: Former German POW Finds Peace in Texas* for the story of a man who later became a U.S. Citizen. The grandson of one of the Italian Generals, Maurizio Parri, published his grandfather's war time diaries in *Il Giuramento; Generale a El Alamein, prigioniero in America (1942-1945).*

Some former POWs have been gracious about allowing interviews at reunions, such as Adriano Angerilli, Enzio Luciolli, Giuseppe Margotilli, and Fernando Togni (pictured above). Some of the former guards, prisoners, and their families have become available for interviews using email, like Ernst Bulkat, Mario Iannantuoni and August Orsini. On other occasions, I'm able to interview the children or grandchildren of a former POW in Italy or the U.S.

In 2009, one of the last reunions of former POWs visited the chapel build by POWs at Camp Hereford, TX. This is indicative of a growing awareness that these memories and relationships must be preserved through reunions, books, lectures, and movies.

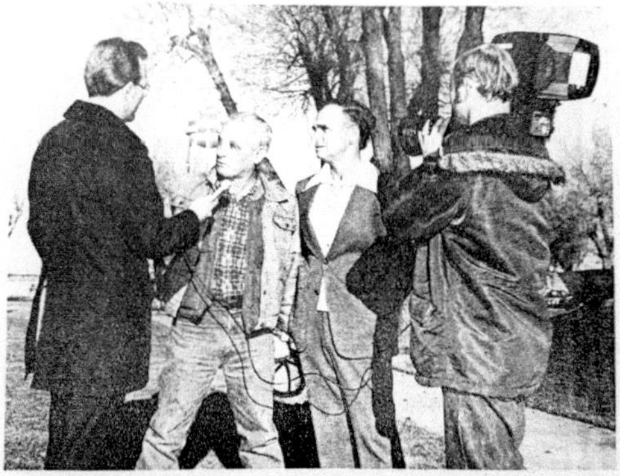

Former POW's Remember

Howard Noel, Channel 5 News Joe Giordana Gene Maconi

Gene Maconi and Joe Giordana took time this week to recount stories of the Italian POW camp which later became a service organization located here during World War II. Channel 5 News stopped by to film the occasion as sites of the old facilities were remembered. Mr. Maconi is the operator of a tile company in Ogden and Mr. Giordana is a Depot employee assigned to the Directorate of Installation Services. Both Mr. Maconi and Mr. Giordana went back to Italy after the war but returned to Ogden to make their homes. Asked why they came back both had the same answer – "To marry a local girl."

Courtesy of Special Collections Department, Stewart Library, Weber State University.

Some local magazines and newspapers have done stories on the camps and published interviews with former POWs returning to visit, or who had moved back to the area where they'd been imprisoned. Some of these have been preserved by the newspaper, some by local historians, colleges, and historical societies.

A documentary video, *Prisoners in Paradise*, directed by Camilla Calamandrei, tells some of the stories of former Italian POWs, a couple from Utah.

Some local TV stations did interviews with surviving former POWs living in their communities in the 1970s and 1980s, like KUED and KSL in Salt Lake City, UT. Some local colleges (Special Collections, Stewart Library, Weber State University) created video archives containing interviews of former POWs and their families and former guards and other employees who had interaction with POWs.

Some former POWs, guards, and their families donated their diaries and photos to local historical societies, like Drew County Historical Museum, Monticello, Arkansas. Some donated to the National Archives (NARA) in College Park, Maryland. Some donated to the Stato Maggiore Esercito in Rome, Italy. I expect more will be found in local colleges and libraries in America, Italy, and Germany.

Former guards, like Thomas Todaro and Peter A. Pulia, Sr. also shared their memories in interviews and photos. Some, like Ralph Storm, wrote books about their experiences with POWs.

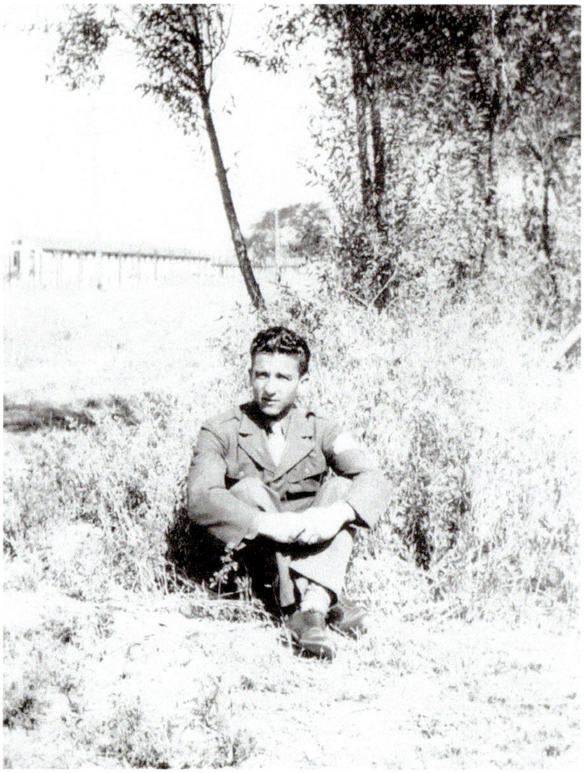

Wilson Longo (named for Woodrow Wilson) was born and died in Bellosguardo, Italy. He was a prisoner at Utah ASF. His cousin, Barbara, provided this photo and information.

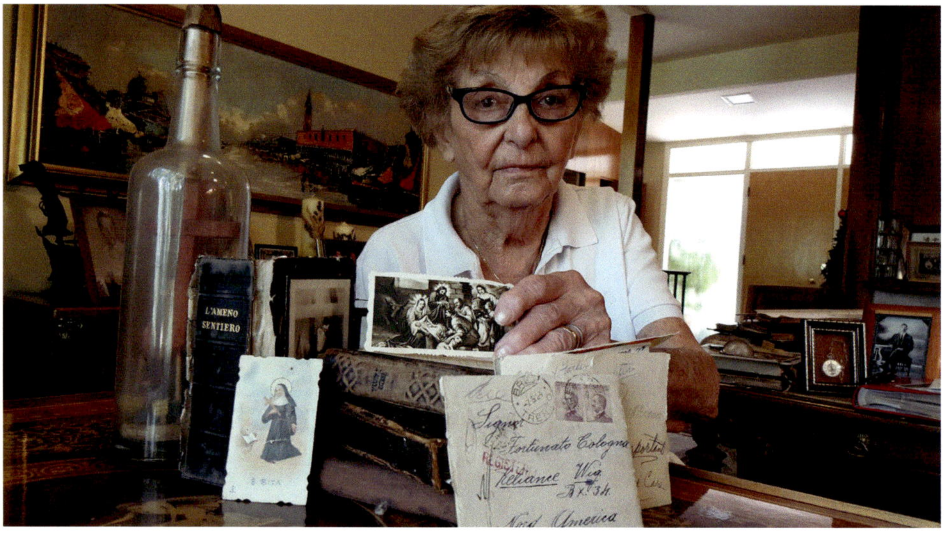

Mary Ravarino with photos and letters from the Italian POWs who worked on her family's farm in Salt Lake City area. Photo courtesy of Italian Center of the West (UtahCulturalNews.com).

Even today, I receive emails from the children and grandchildren of former POWs to learn more about the experiences of being a POW in the U.S. and the hope of locating records regarding their work, health, and transfers. Most of these former POWs don't/didn't talk about their experiences. Mario Turrini only told his children that Hawaii was nice, with no comment on his service in Greece, Tunisia, or his experiences at the other camps where he was held in the U.S.

Some of these letters come from Italy, but some also come from England, Australia, and the United States where these men took their families after the war.

These memories can assist us in planning for the future, and promoting the preservation of photos and artifacts from the POW camps. Preservation of these memories can also be achieved by conducting interviews of surviving former POWs and their guards, and members of the community.

We can use these memories and memorabilia to educate public about the policies and experiences of WWII and to promote the good treatment of future POWs.

POW Camps by Location

There were 1,204 Prisoner of War Camps, Italian Service Unit Camps, and Prisoner of War hospitals in the U.S.

The camp lists at NARA shows several APO addresses in place of camp names. Judging by the dates, these were located in the Philippines, Hawaii, and New Caledonia.

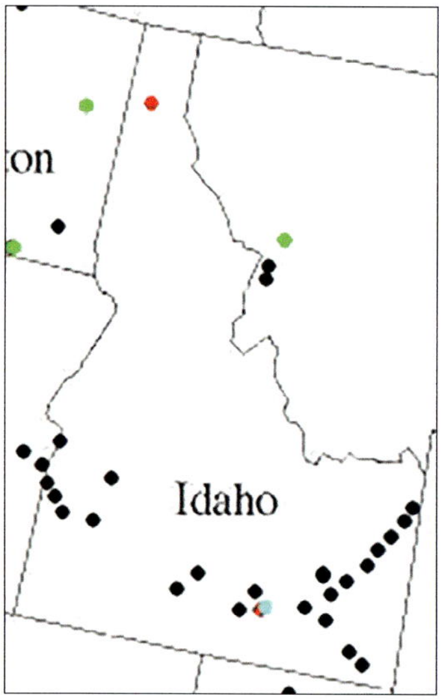

Courtesy of John Saffell.

In Idaho, there were 16,970 German POWS in 21 POW camps as follows:

Aberdeen, Bingham County, ID (branch camp under Rupert). This camp opened on 18 October 1944. At maximum, it held 531 German POWs on 16 October 1945. They were doing agricultural work.

Blackfoot, Bingham County, ID (branch camp under Rupert). This camp opened on 1 October 1944. At maximum, it held 500 German POWs on 1 October 1944. They were doing agricultural work.

Emmett, Gem County, ID (branch camp under Rupert). This camp opened on 16 September 1945. At maximum, it held 260 German POWs. They were doing agricultural work.

Farragut (David) Naval Training Station, Athol, Kootenai County, ID (base camp), now Farragut State Park. This camp opened for POWs on 8 March 1945 and was primarily a training camp, with the POW labor used for landscaping and building maintenance as well as agricultural work in local farms and canneries. At maximum, it held 838 German POWs on 1 August 1945.

Filer, Twin Falls County, ID (branch camp under Rupert). This camp opened on 1 June 1945. At maximum, it held 350 German POWs on 1 June 1945. They were doing agricultural work.

Fort Hall, Bannock and Bingham Counties, ID, on Indian reservation land plus part of Pocatello city (branch camp under Rupert). This camp opened on 8 October 1944. At maximum, it held 346 German POWs on 8 October 1944. They were doing agricultural work. The camp was located where the new Fort Hall High School is now.

Camp Franklin, Nampa, Franklin County, ID (branch camp under Rupert) (see Nampa). This camp was established by the farmers in the community to offset the labor shortage. It opened on 1 June 1945. At maximum, it held 377 German POWs on 1 November1945. They lived in tents and worked in agriculture.

Holly Lake (Camp), Minidoka County, ID (branch camp under Rupert). This camp opened on 23 June 1945. At maximum, it held 225 German POWs employed in agricultural work.

Idaho Falls, Bonneville County, ID (branch camp under Rupert). This camp opened on 1 October 1944. At maximum, it held 733 German POWs work in agriculture on 16 October 1945.

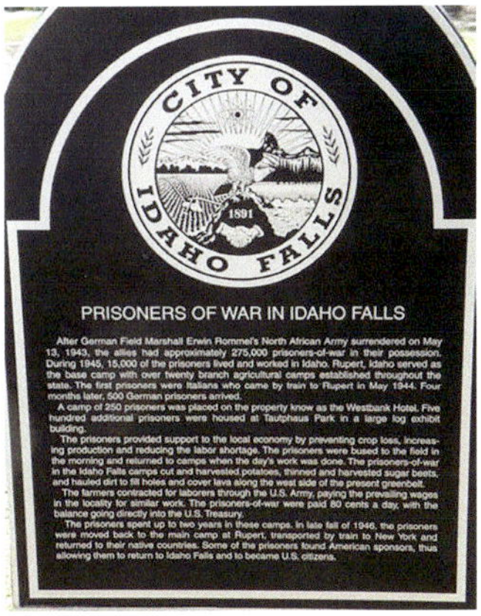

http://www.waymarking.com/waymarks/WMC5YC_Prisoners_of_War_in_Idaho_Falls.

Jerome, Jerome County, ID (branch camp under Rupert). This camp opened on 15 May 1945. At maximum, it held 224 German POWs working in agriculture on 15 June 1945.

Marsing, Owyhee County, ID (branch camp under Rupert). This camp opened on 1 June 1945. At maximum, it held 250 German POWs working in agriculture on 1 June 1945.

Nampa, Canyon County, ID (see Franklin)

Paul, Minidoka County, ID (see Rupert)

Payette, Payette County, ID (branch camp under Rupert). The camp opened on 16 September 1945. At maximum, it held 242 German POWs working in agriculture on the same date.

Pocatello, Bannock County, ID (branch camp under Rupert). This camp opened on 1 October 1945. At maximum, it held 993 German POWs on 15 December 1945, working in agriculture.

Preston, Franklin County, ID (branch camp under Rupert). This camp opened on 8 June 1945. At maximum, it held 250 German POWs on 16 September 1945, working in agriculture.

Rigby, Jefferson County, ID (branch camp under Rupert). This camp opened on 8 October 1944. At maximum, it held 429 German POWs on 1 October 1945, working in agriculture.

Rupert (Camp), Rupert, Minidoka County, ID (base camp, see Paul). This camp opened on 24 October 1943. At maximum, it held 8,477 German POWs on 1 July 1945. They worked in military and agricultural jobs.

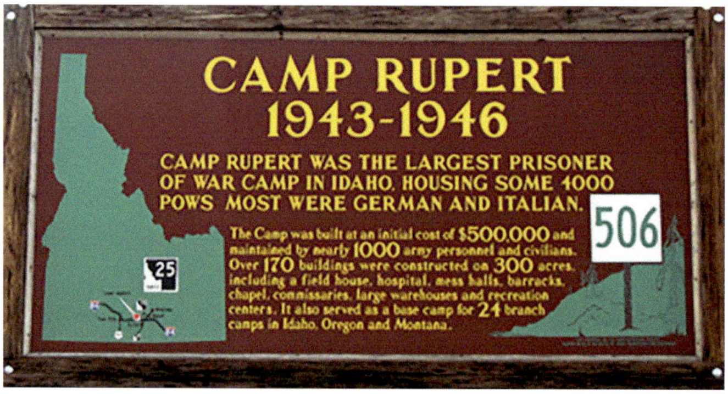

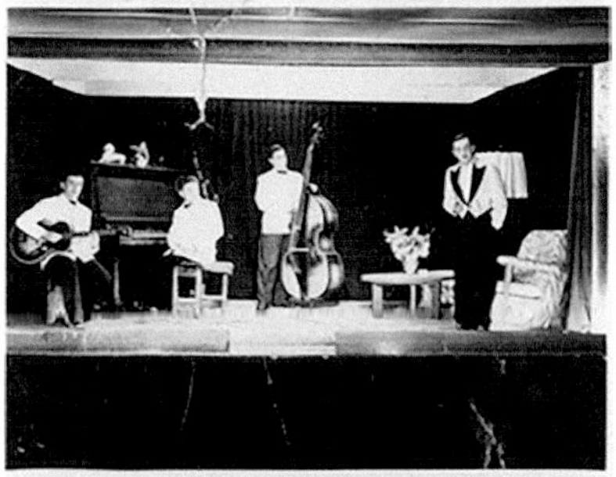

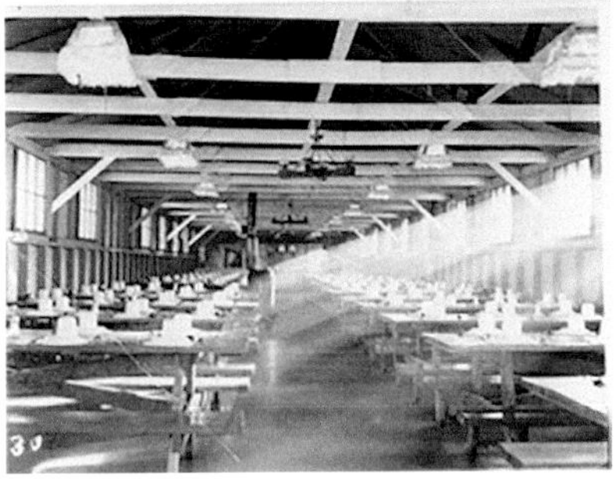

http://magicvalley.com/news/local/historical-marker-placed-at-wwii-pow-camp-rupert/article_ca518126-6807-539c-bc9b-af8327ead5a4.html.

Shelley, Bingham County, ID (branch camp under Rupert). This camp opened on 16 October 1945. At maximum, it held 385 German POWs on 1 November 1945. They worked in agricultural jobs.

Sugar City, Madison County, ID (branch camp under Rupert). This camp opened on 16 October 1945. At maximum, it held 344 German POWs working in agricultural jobs.

Thomas, Bingham County, ID (branch camp under Rupert). This camp opened on 16 October 1945. At maximum, it held 295 German POWs on 1 November 1945, working in agricultural jobs.

Upper Deer Flat, Canyon County, ID (branch camp under Rupert). This camp opened on 1 June 1945. At maximum, it held 235 German POWs on 1 November 1945, working in agricultural jobs.

Wilder, Canyon County, ID (branch camp under Rupert). This camp opened on 16 May 1945. At maximum, it held 696 German POWs on 15 December 1945, working in agricultural jobs.

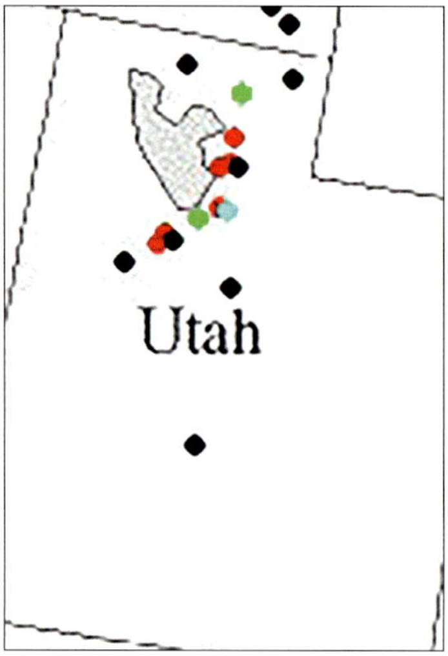

Courtesy of John Saffell.

In Utah, there were German (10,823), Italian (8,162) and Japanese (23) POWs at fourteen locations as follows:

Bushnell (George E.) General Hospital, Brigham City, Box Elder County, UT. This POW camp opened on 1 January 1944.

This was one of the Army regional hospitals established around the county. The POWs were in their own wing of the hospital. At maximum, there were:
75 German POW patients here in April 1945
49 Italian POW Patients here in May 1945
23 Japanese POW patients here in June 1944

Also, POWs worked at this location:
301 Italian POWs in April 1945
334 German POWs in October 1945.

Clearfield Naval Supply Depot, Clearfield, Davis County, UT (base camp). This POW camp opened on 8 May 1945. It was a set of warehouses for the effects of American servicemen who died in the Pacific until they could be returned to their families. At maximum, there were:
301 Italian POWs in April 1945
334 German POWs in October 1945.

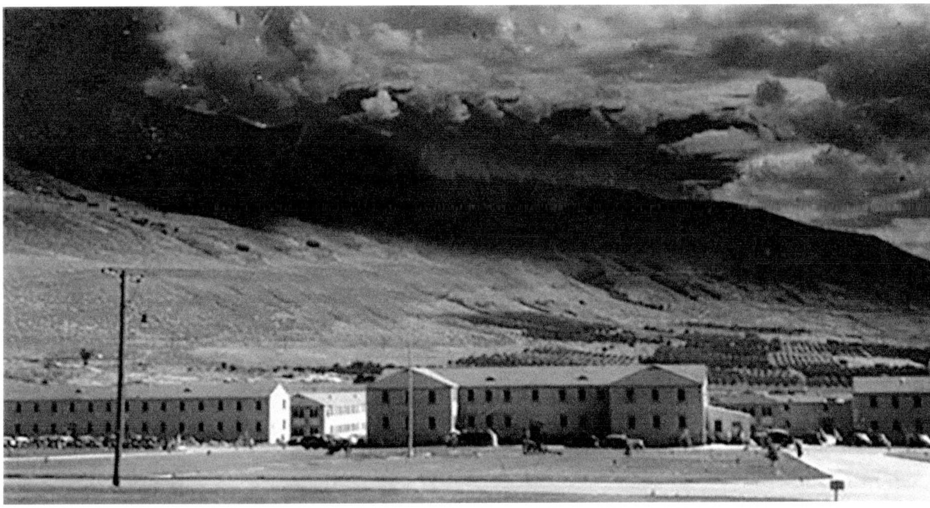

Bushnell General Hospital, Brigham City, UT, from http://history.amedd.army.mil, accessed February 2017.

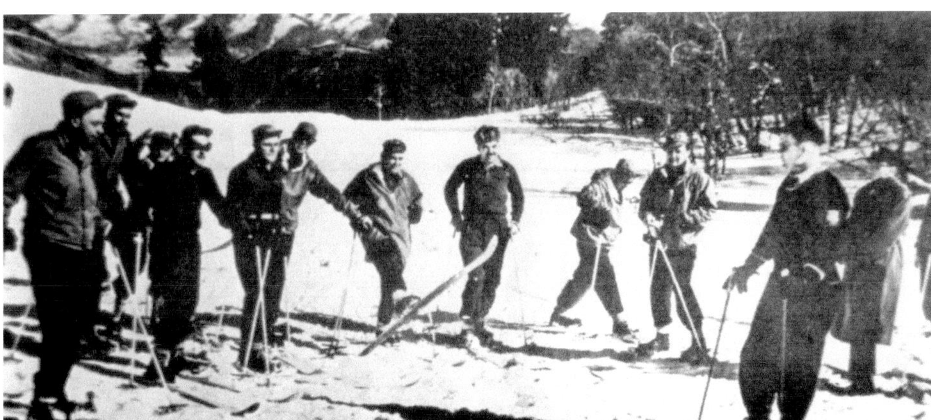

Rehabilitation at Snowbasin, out of Bushnell General Hospital, Brigham City, UT, photo courtesy of Special Collections Department, Stewart Library, Weber State University. Italian POWs built this facility for use by American GIs.

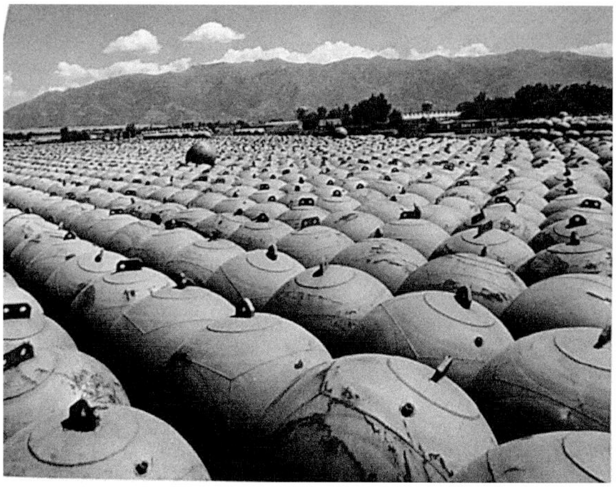
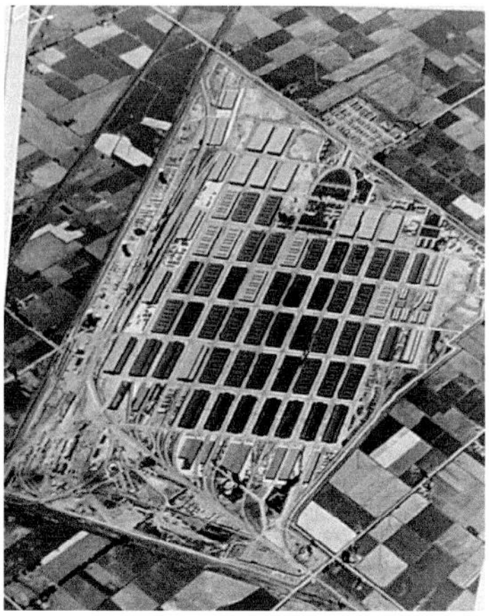

Ball field and overview of Clearfield Naval Supply Station, Clearfield, UT from National Archives and Records Administration, Denver, CO.

Deseret Chemical Weapons Depot, Tooele, Tooele County, UT, (ISU). This POW camp opened on 1 January 1944. It was warehouse work for the military effort. At maximum, there were:
1,160 German POWs in January 1944
117 Italian Service Unit members in September 1945

This location is still an active military reservation, no photos.

Douglas (Fort Stephen A.), Salt Lake City, Salt Lake County, UT (base camp). The POW camp opened on 1 July 1945. The work for POWs here was primarily grounds work and building maintenance. The headquarters for the 9th Service Command was moved here from The Presidio in San Francisco shortly after December 7, 1941. The prisoners were held at the old WWI POW camp (crew of the German ship *Cormoran* built many of the barracks), later used as a CCC camp, on the edge of the Fort's land. At maximum, there were:
184 Italian POWs in April 1945
233 German POWs in May 1945

Dugway Proving Grounds, Dugway, Tooele County, UT (branch camp under Warner, ISU). This POW camp opened on 23 May 1945. At maximum, there were:
100 Italian POWs in May 1945
103 Italian Service Unit members in September 1945

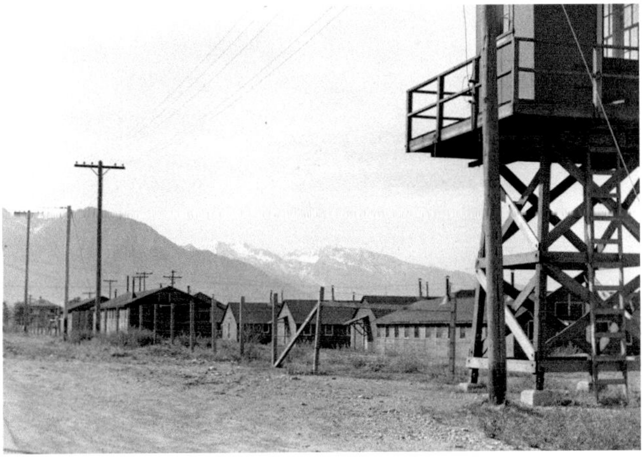

POW housing at Fort Douglas, UT, used with permission, Utah Historical Society.

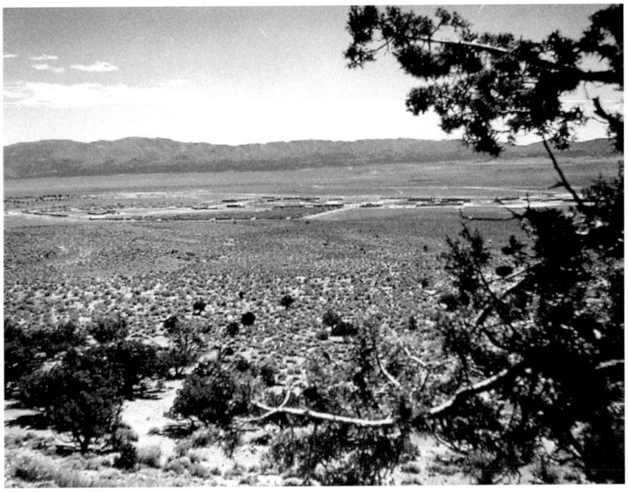

Overview of Dugway, courtesy of Special Collections Department, Stewart Library, Weber State University.

This location is still an active military reservation, but we located one photo of Dugway.

Hill Field (SCU 1935), Weber and Davis Counties, UT (base camp), now Hill Air Force Base. This POW camp opened on 15 February 1944. At maximum, there were:
1,231 Italian POWs in March 1945

This location is still an active military reservation, no exterior photos.

Kearns AAF Regional Station Hospital, Kearns, Salt Lake County, UT. This location only held the 28 German POWs shot at Salina on 8 July 1945, with the exception of the seven who died before arrival and the one who went to Bushnell for advanced care and

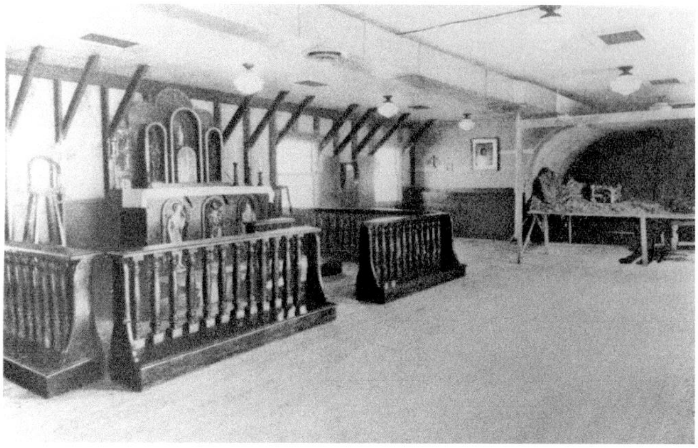

POW chapel at Hill Field, used with permission, Utah Historical Society.

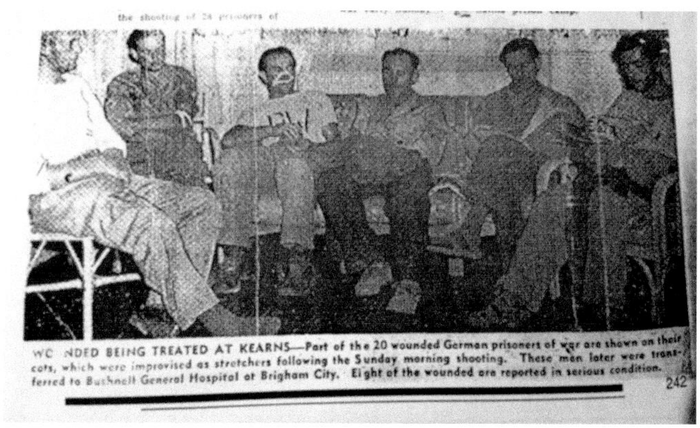

WOUNDED BEING TREATED AT KEARNS—Part of the 20 wounded German prisoners of war are shown on their cots, which were improvised as stretchers following the Sunday morning shooting. These men later were transferred to Bushnell General Hospital at Brigham City. Eight of the wounded are reported in serious condition.

242

Newspaper photo of German POW patients at Kearns Naval Station Hospital, Special Collections Department, Stewart Library, Weber State University.

eventually died there. Only one of the men here died. His brain injuries were too severe to move him to Bushnell and his care was primarily pain management until his death a week later. It is now the South Valley Regional Airport.

Logan, Cache County, UT (branch camp under Ogden ASF Depot). The POW camp opened on 8 June 1945. They lived at the fairgrounds and in the dormitories of Utah State College to bring in crops in the area. At maximum, there were:
400 German POWs in June 1945

Ogden Arsenal, Ogden, Weber County, UT (ISU). This facility was located at the mouth of the canyon on land now part of Hill Air Force Base. It opened as a POW camp on 1 October 1945. The POWs worked on local farms. At maximum, there were:
668 Italian POWs in October 1945

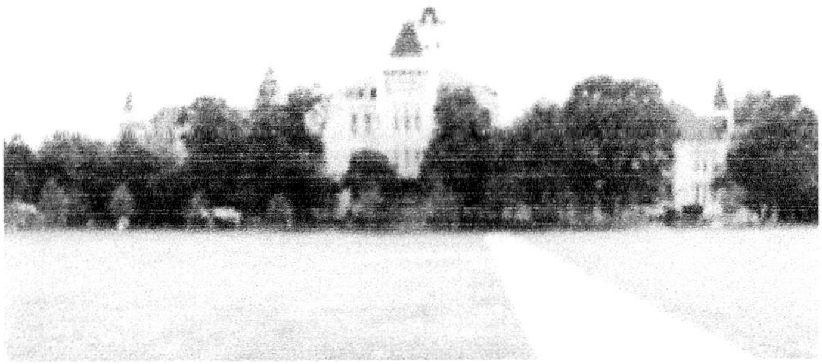

https://www.usu.edu/.

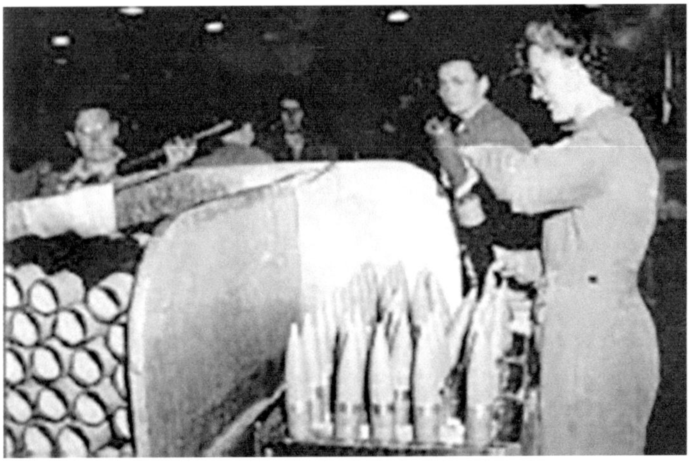

Inside Ogden Arsenal (right), overview (below) from NARA Denver.

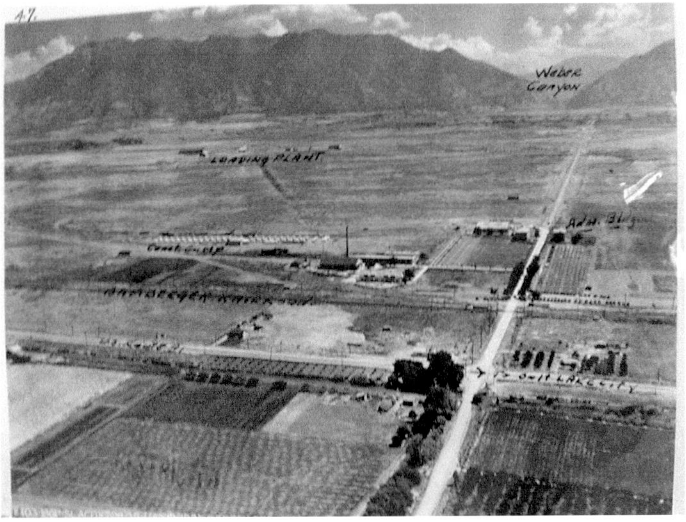

Utah ASF Depot, Ogden, Weber County, UT (ISU). This base camp opened on 7 October 1942. Work here ranged from Quartermaster Supply to work on local farms and canneries to work for the Ogden Chamber of Commerce. It was later called Ogden Defense Depot. At maximum, there were:

4,481 Italian POWs in May 1944

5,006 German POWs in August 1945

1,767 Italian Service Unit members in September 1945

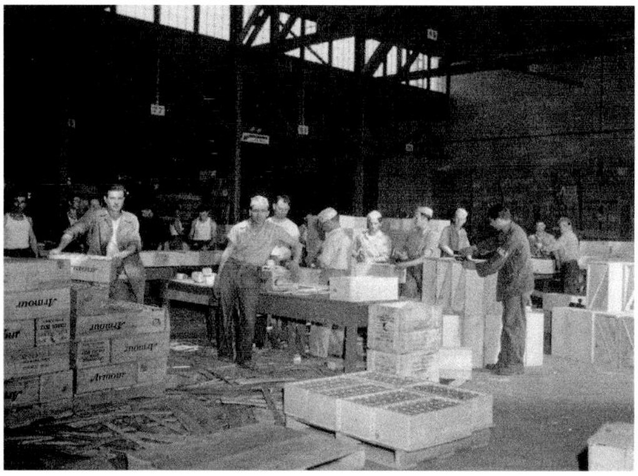

Utah ASF Depot, Ogden, UT, courtesy of Special Collections Department, Stewart Library, Weber State University.

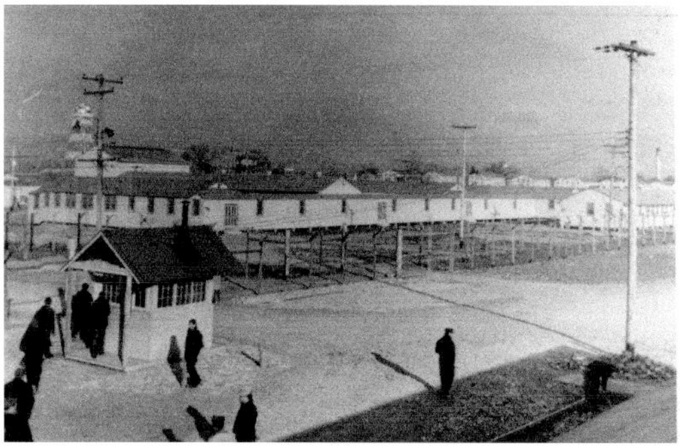

Utah ASF Depot Main Gate (left) and POW yard (below), courtesy of Special Collections Department, Stewart Library, Weber State University.

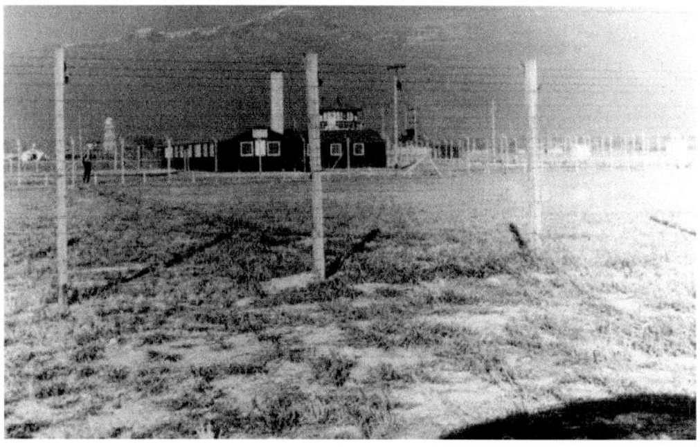

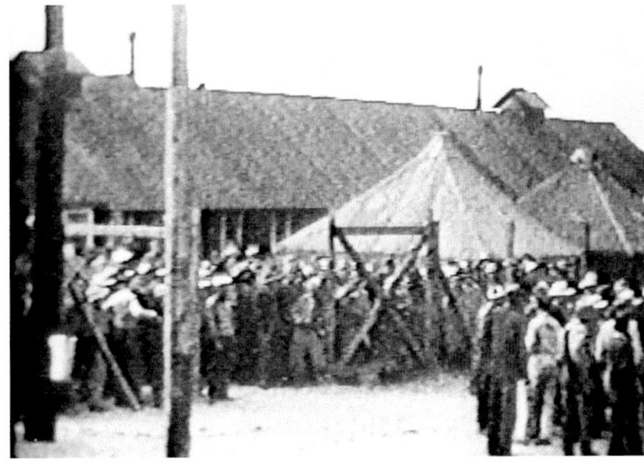

Orem POW Camp, https://www.scera.org/orem-heritage-museum/.

Orem, Utah County, UT (branch camp under Ogden ASF Depot). The POW camp opened on 1 July 1945. They were doing primarily farm work while living here. At maximum, there were:
325 German POWs in November 1945

Salina, Sevier County, UT (branch camp under Ogden ASF Depot) (former CCC camp). This camp opened on 23 June 1944. It was a temporary tent camp for the harvest. This location is infamous for the shooting of prisoners by a guard at midnight on 8 July 1945. 28 POWs were wounded, 9 of whom died. At maximum, there were:
250 German POWs in June 1945

Tooele Ordnance Depot, Tooele, Tooele County, UT (see Warner)

Tremonton, Box Elder County, UT (branch camp under Ogden ASF Depot). The POW camp opened on 8 June 1945. They worked here on the farms. At maximum, there were:

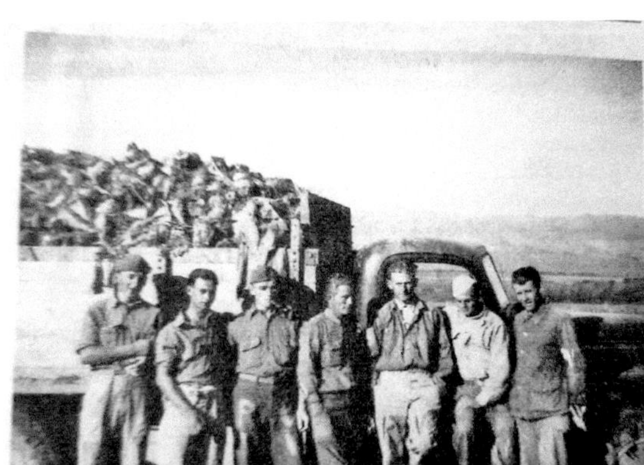

Salina POW farm workers, http://salinasunonline.com/ccc-pow-camp-salina-utah-museum/.

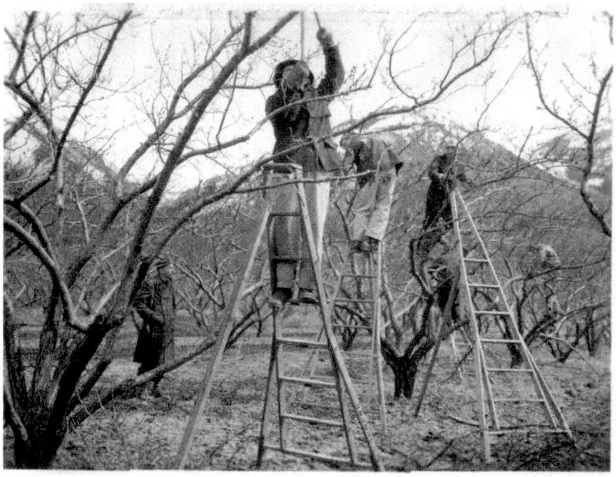

Pruning an orchard in Tremonton, courtesy of Special Collections Department, Stewart Library, Weber State University.

383 German POWs in December 1945

Warner (Camp), Tooele Ordnance Depot, Tooele, Tooele County, UT (ISU) (see Tooele). This military location grew from the original Camp Warner. It opened for POWs on 1 February 1944. Prisoners did warehouse and farm work here. At maximum, there were:
2,200 German POWs in January 1944
928 Italian POWs in December 1945

This location is still an active military reservation, no photos.

Death Index

There was a total of 901 Germans (includes three Russians, four Austrians, one Yugoslavian, one Czech, and one Turk), 172 Italians, and 23 Japanese (includes one Korean) out of 1,175 POWs who died while held in the U.S. during WWI & WWII. The following seven men died in Idaho and 53 men died in Utah and were buried at Fort Douglas Post Cemetery where all but one can be found today:

Barilaro, Luigi, died at Bushnell General Hospital on 30 May 1941, buried at Fort Douglas, UT
Behr, Felix, World War I, died and buried at Fort Douglas, UT, civilian
Benes, Frank, World War I, died and buried at Fort Douglas, UT, civilian
Blaase, Karl G. W., World War I, died and buried at Fort Douglas, UT, civilian
Bonasora, Ignazio, died at Ogden Depot on 2 October 1945, buried at Fort Douglas, UT
Bross, Otto, died at Salina on 8 July 1945, buried at Fort Douglas, UT
Burke, Frank R., World War I, died at Fort Douglas, UT, buried in Chicago, IL, civilian
Canevari, Luigi, died in Idaho on 9 July 1944, in transit from Fort Lawton, WA, to Ogden, buried at Fort Douglas, UT
Cantello, Salvatore, died at Bushnell General Hospital on 26 February 1945, buried at Fort Douglas, UT
Cincotta, Giovanni, died at Ogden Arsenal on 8 August 1945, buried at Fort Douglas, UT
D'Augenti, Nicola, died at Ogden Depot on 27 August 1943, buried at Fort Douglas, UT
Eilert, Paul, died at Bushnell General Hospital on 8 June 1944, buried at Fort Douglas, UT
Felgenhauer, Johann ... (died in Bonneville county on 16 October 1945, buried at Rupert, ID, transferred to Golden Gate National Cemetery, CA)
Forzellin, Bruno, died at Ogden Depot on 9 December 1945, buried at Fort Douglas, UT
Fuchs, Ernst, died at Salina on 8 July 1945, buried at Fort Douglas, UT
Fuckola, Joseph, World War I, died and buried at Fort Douglas, UT, civilian
Gaag, Gottfried, died at Salina on 8 July 1945, buried at Fort Douglas, UT
Gabriel, Hans, died at Ogden Depot on 13 August 1945, buried at Fort Douglas, UT
German, Herman, World War I, died and buried at Fort Douglas, UT, civilian
Hanf, Friedrich O., World War I, died and buried at Fort Douglas, UT, civilian
Heimerdinger, Paul, died at Ogden Depot on 13 September 1945, buried at Fort Douglas, UT
Heinrich, Karl, died at Bushnell General Hospital on 6 August 1945, buried at Fort Douglas, UT
Indomenico, Sebastiano, died at Bushnell General Hospital on 10 June 1944, buried at Fort Douglas, UT
Kampmann, Maximilian, World War I, died and buried at Fort Douglas, UT, civilian

Kontowski, Erich Paul ... (died in Twin Falls county on 23 November 1945,buried at Rupert, ID, transferred to Golden Gate National Cemetery, CA)
Laevemann, Erich, World War I, died and buried at Fort Douglas, UT, civilian
Laschke, Emil, World War I, died and buried at Fort Douglas, UT
Leopold, Max, World War I, died and buried at Fort Douglas, UT, civilian
Lewitski, Stanilaus, World War I, died and buried at Fort Douglas, UT, POW
Lieder, Herman, World War I, died and buried at Fort Douglas, UT, civilian
Liske, Georg, died at Salina on 8 July 1945, buried at Fort Douglas, UT
Maas, Hermann, died at Ogden Depot on 15 July 1945, buried at Fort Douglas, UT
Malinowski, Alfred, died at Ogden Depot on 27 September 1944, buried at Fort Douglas, UT
Meli, Angelo, died at Bushnell General Hospital on 4 December 1944, buried at Fort Douglas, UT
Meyer, Hans, died at Salina on 8 July 1945, buried at Fort Douglas, UT
Morth, Charles, World War I, died and buried at Fort Douglas, UT, civilian
Nedbal, Otto ... (died in Minidoka county on 3 December 1945, buried at Rupert, ID, transferred to Golden Gate National Cemetery, CA)
Nedell, Wilhelm... (died at Burley on 19 June 1946, buried at Rupert, ID, transferred to Golden Gate National Cemetery, CA)
Paul, Adolf, died at Salina on 8 July 1945, buried at Fort Douglas, UT
Pazzi, Vincenzo, died at Ogden Depot on 28 August 1945, buried at Fort Douglas, UT
Piezareck, Walter J., World War I, died and buried at Fort Douglas, UT, civilian
Rabbai, Francesco, died at Bushnell General Hospital on 20 May 1945, UT, buried at Fort Douglas, UT
Rascher, Heinz, died at Bushnell General Hospital on 20 July 1945, buried at Fort Douglas, UT
Raschke, Erich, died at Ogden Depot on 28 August 1945, buried at Fort Douglas, UT
Ritter, Friedrich, died at Kearns AAF Regional Hospital on 13 July 1945, buried at Fort Douglas, UT
Ruebe, Arthur, World War I, died and buried at Fort Douglas, UT, civilian
Ruffino, Francesco, died at Ogden Depot on 7 June 1945, buried at Fort Douglas, UT
Schaefer, Karl, died at Bushnell General Hospital on 5 May 1945, buried at Fort Douglas, UT
Schmidt, Georg, World War I, died and buried at Fort Douglas, UT, civilian
Schmidt, Paul Rudi ... (died at Pocatello on 14 September 1944, buried at Rupert, ID, transferred to Golden Gate National Cemetery, CA)
Shibata, Shigeo, died at Bushnell General Hospital on 31 July 1944, buried at Fort Douglas, UT
Stadler, Frank, World War I, died and buried at Fort Douglas, UT, civilian
Stockmann, Fritz, died at Salina on 8 July1945, buried at Fort Douglas, UT
Topff, Walter, World War I, died and buried at Fort Douglas, UT, civilian
Vogel, Walter, died at Salina on 8 July 1945, buried at Fort Douglas, UT
Wachenhusen, Adolf, World War I, died and buried at Fort Douglas, UT, civilian
Wieland, Hans, died at Bushnell General Hospital on 30 January 1946, buried at Fort Douglas, UT
Wiemken, Fritz, died at Bushnell General Hospital on 28 January 1945, buried at Fort Douglas, UT
Wude, Henrich ... (died in Minidoka county on 30 October 1944, buried at Rupert, ID, transferred to Golden Gate National Cemetery, CA)
Zilko, Roko, World War I, died and buried at Fort Douglas, UT, civilian
Zinnel, Henry L., World War I, died and buried at Fort Douglas, UT, civilian

Burial Locations List

Place of Burial (in the United States): A total of 91 U.S. Military and civilian cemeteries contained POW burials.

Idaho

Camp Rupert, ID (p. 51A), (six German WWII POW burials transferred to Golden Gate National Cemetery in CA)

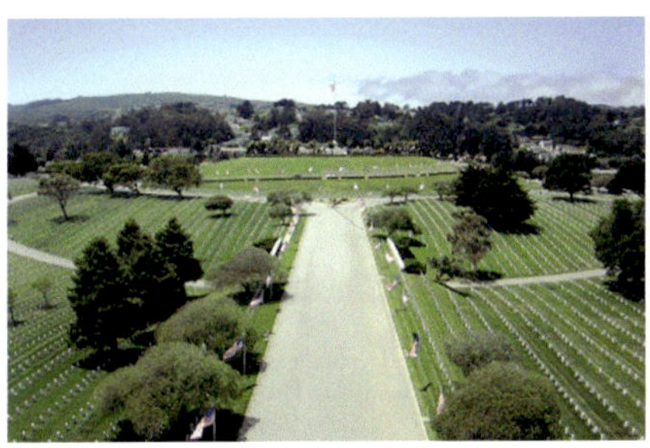

https://www.cem.va.gov/cems/nchp/goldengate.asp.

Utah

Fort Douglas Post Cemetery, Salt Lake City, UT. The cemetery contains one Japanese, twenty German, and twelve Italian WWII POW burials, plus two WWI POW and nineteen WWI enemy alien burials. This is a federal property on the campus of the University of Utah.

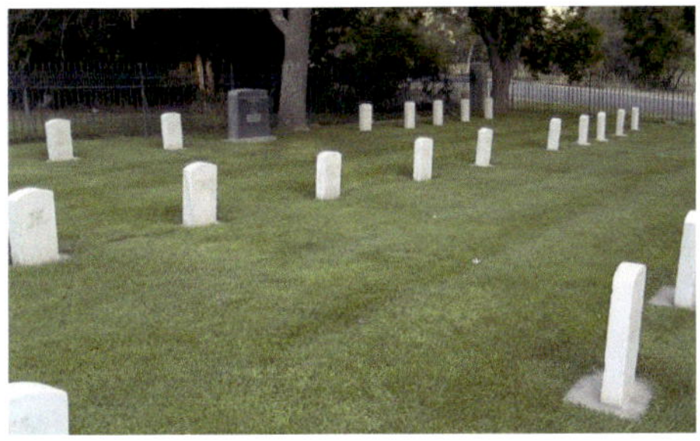

Photo by author.

Appendix A

POW Labor

Photos from NARA, College Park, MD

PRISONERS OF WAR WORK

CLOTHING AND EQUIPMENT

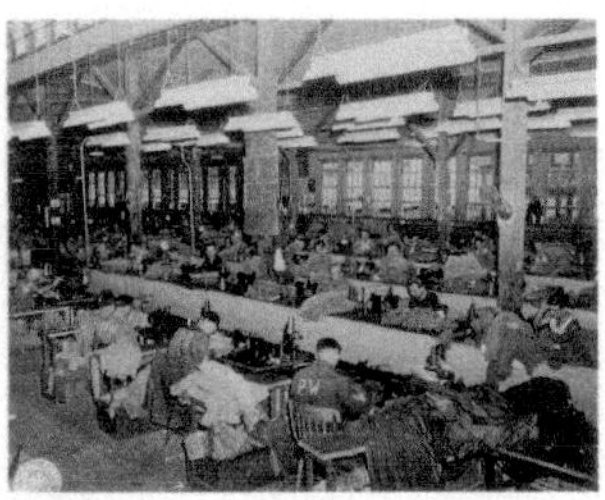

FORT MEADE, MD.

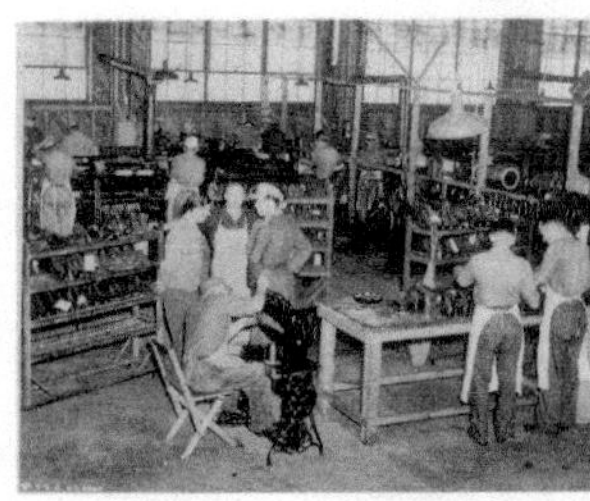

CAMP BLANDING, FLA.

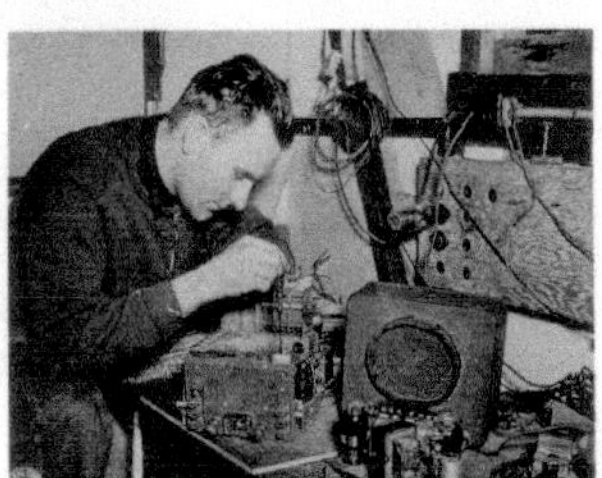

FORT McCLELLAN, ALA.

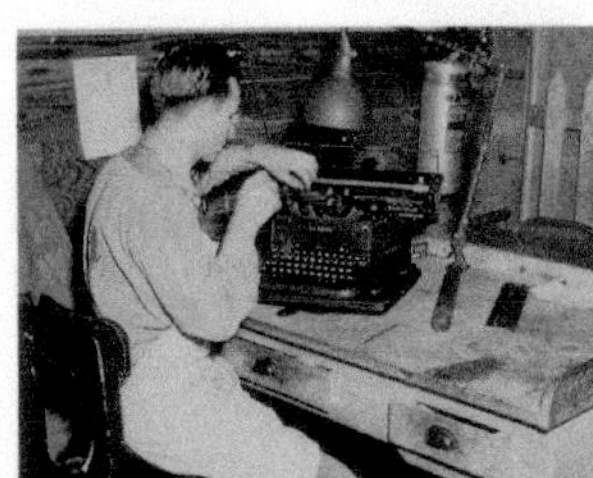

CAMP BRECKINRIDGE, KY.

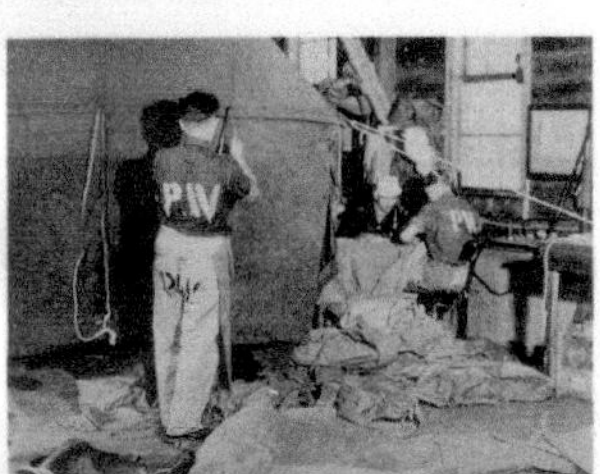

FORT OGELTHORPE, GA.

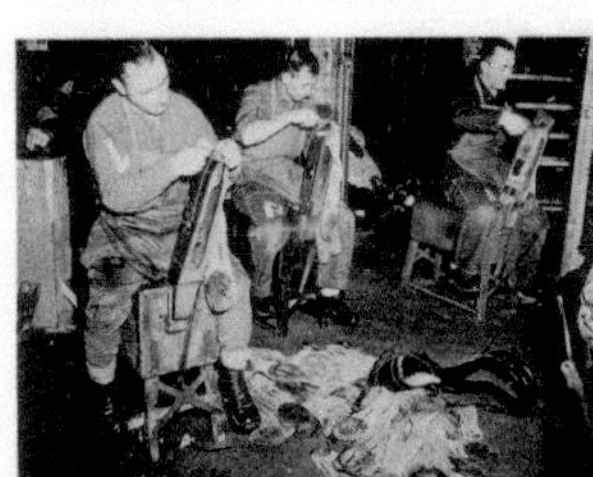

CAMP CARSON, COLO.

WD – ASF – PMGO

PRISONERS OF WAR WORK

MOTOR MAINTENANCE

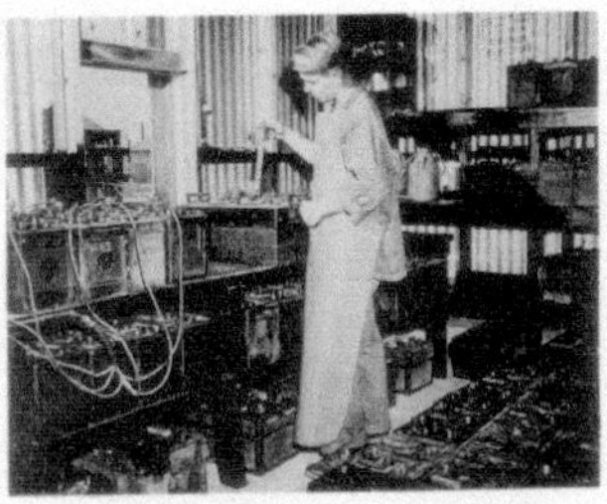

FT. DIX, N. J.

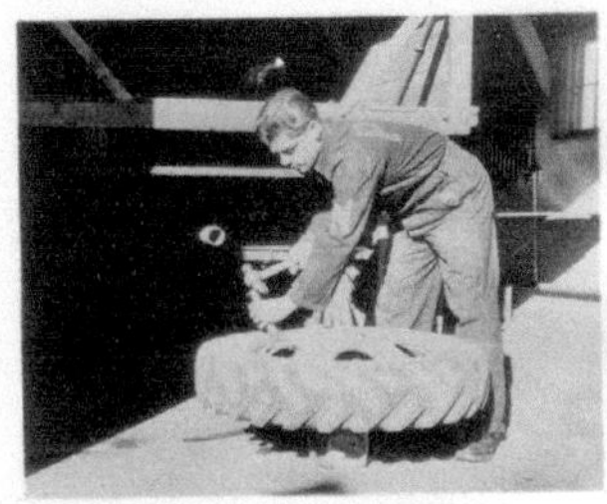

FORT ROBINSON, NEB.

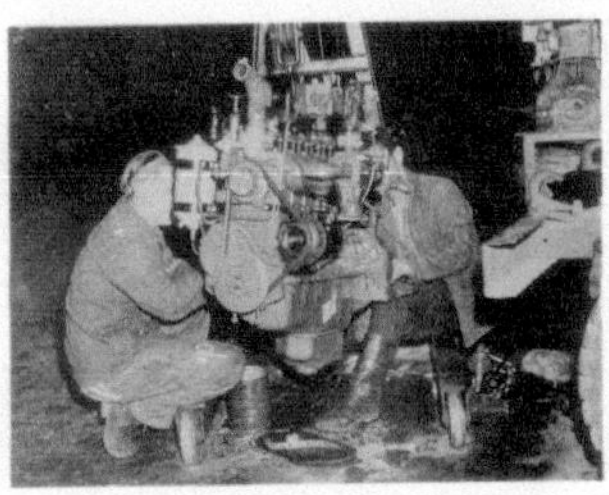

FORT KNOX, KY.

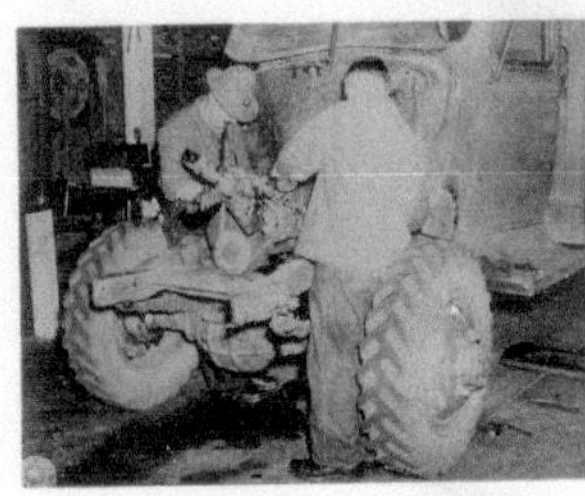

FORT DIX, N. J.

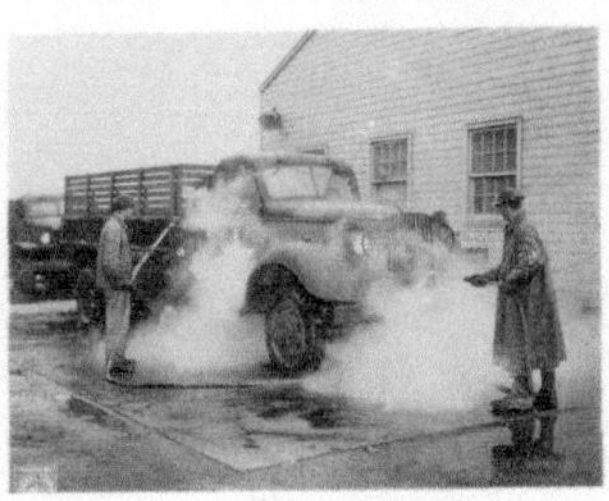

CAMP CAMPBELL, KY.

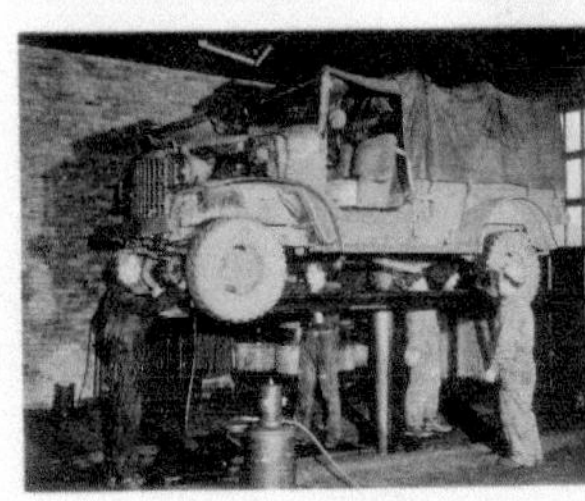

FT. BRAGG, N. C.

WD - ASF - PMGO

PRISONERS OF WAR WORK

REPAIRS AND UTILITIES

FOLLOWING LIST OF SUGGESTED REPAIRS AND UTILITIES OCCUPATIONS FOR PRISONERS OF WAR WAS PREPARED BY OFFICE OF THE CHIEF OF ENGINEERS

SPECIFICATION NUMBER (TM-5-487) OCCUPATION

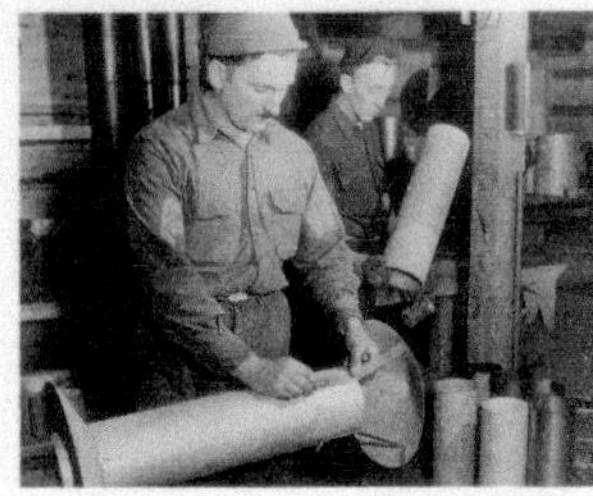

CAMP CLARK, MO.

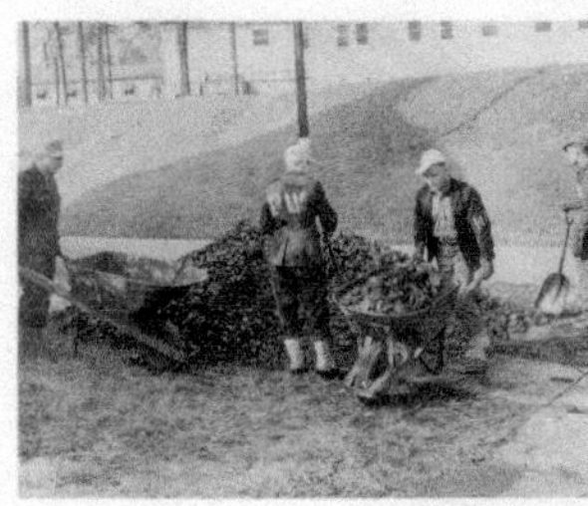

FORT OGELTHORPE, GA.

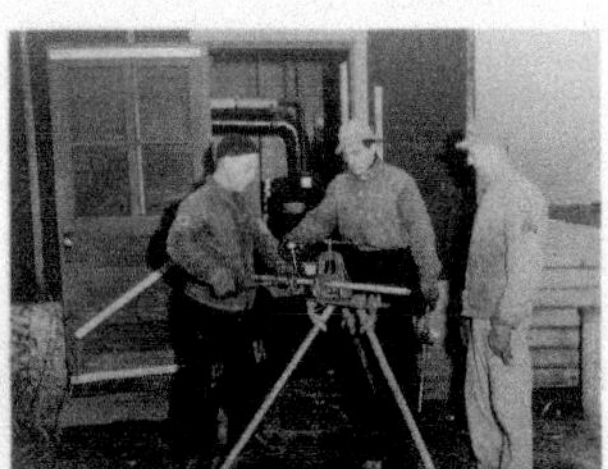

CAMP CLARK, MO.

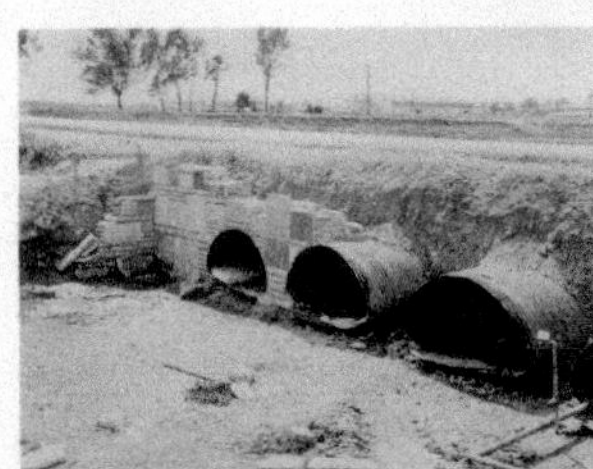

FORT LEONARD WOOD, MO.

WD - ASF - PMGO

PRISONERS OF WAR WORK

POST ENGINEER WORK

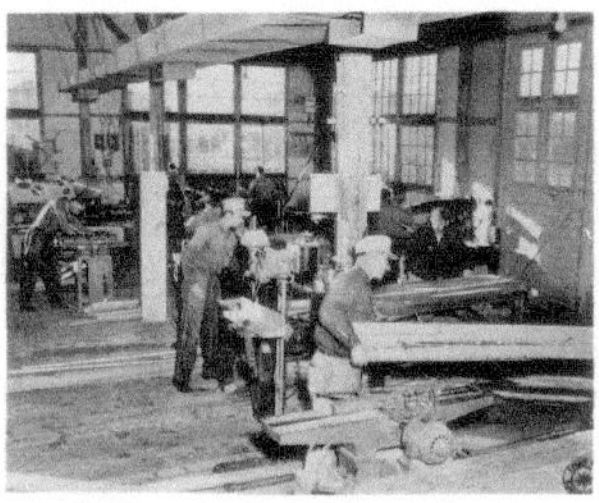

CAMP TRINIDAD, COLO.

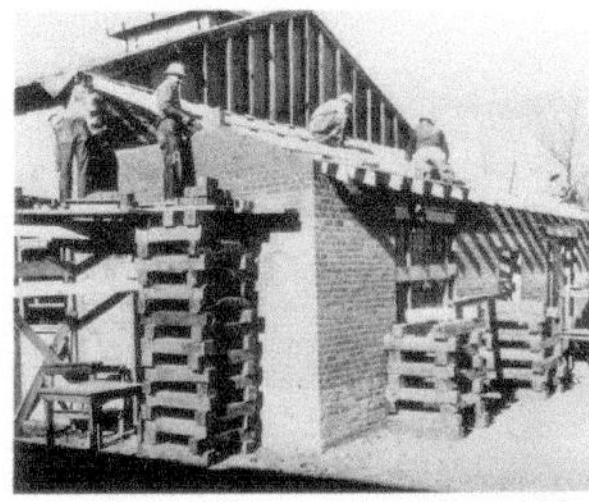

CAMP SHELBY, MISS.

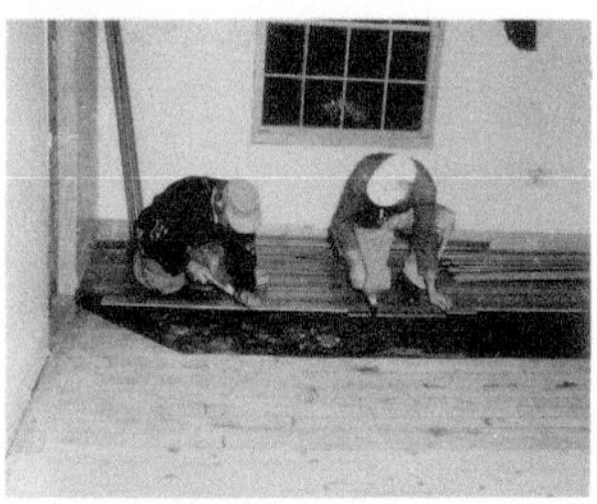

FORT LEONARD WOOD, MO.

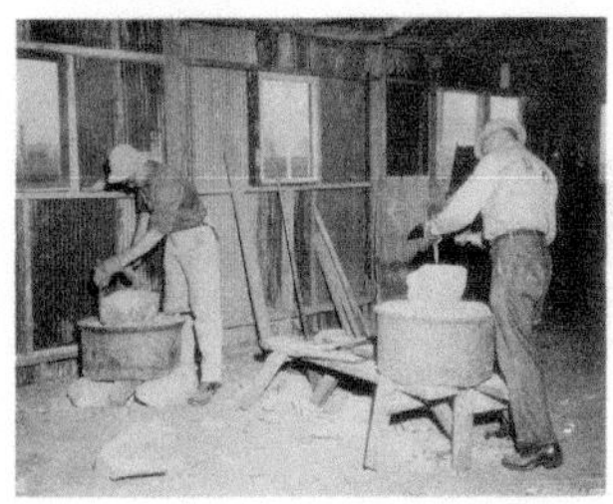

CAMP BRECKINRIDGE, KY.

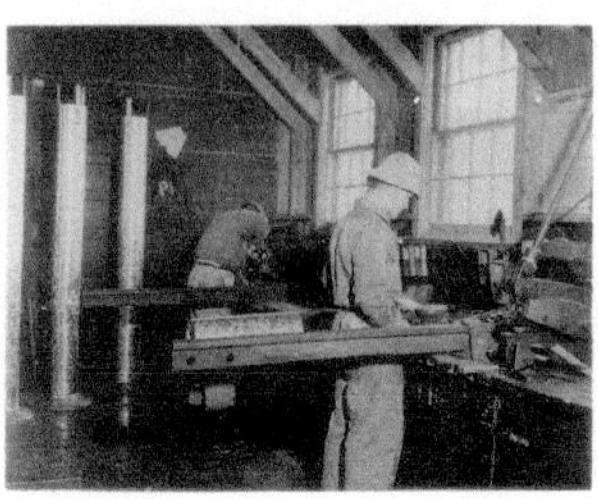

CAMP BRECKINRIDGE, KY.

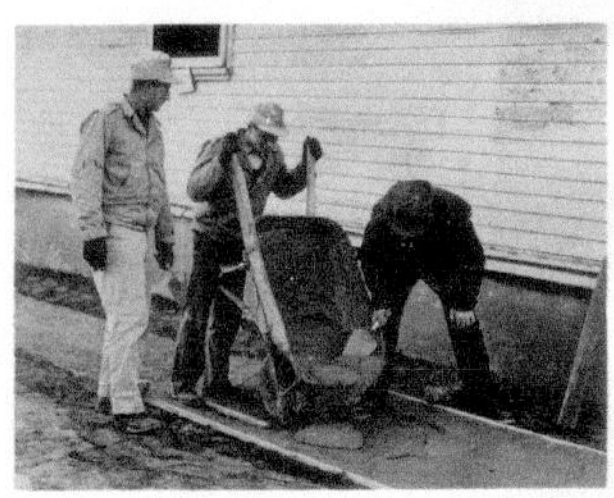

CAMP WHEELER, GA.

WD – ASF – PMGO

PRISONERS OF WAR WORK

POST ENGINEER WORK

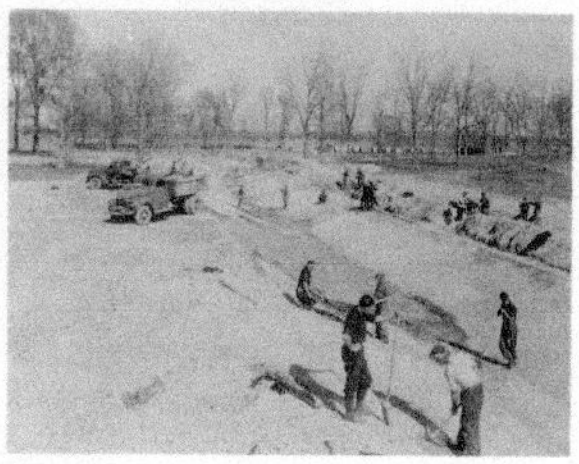

CAMP CLINTON, MISS.

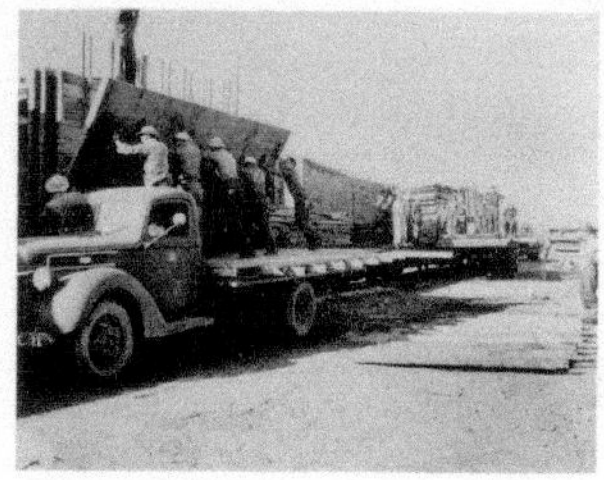

CAMP SUTTON, N. C.

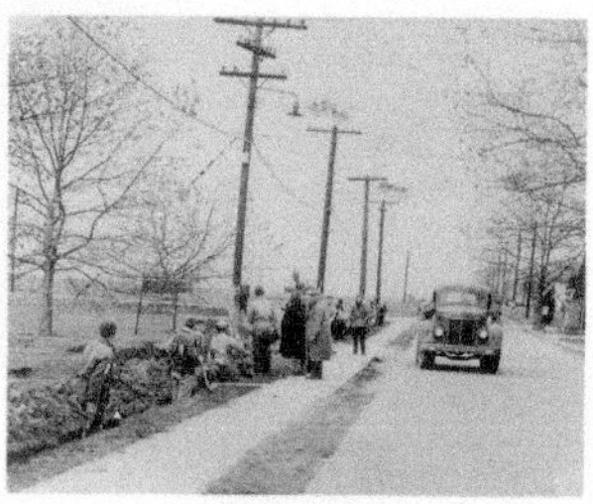

EDGEWOOD ARSENAL, MD.

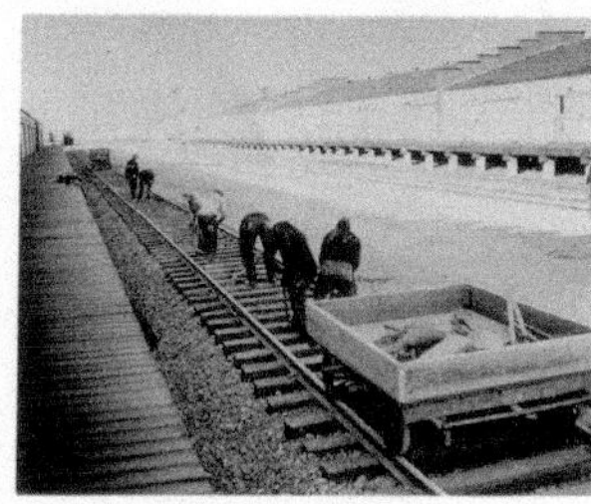

CAMP CARSON, COLO.

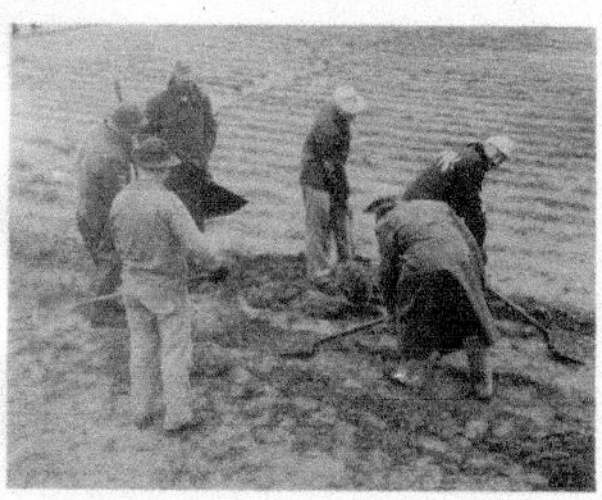

GALVESTON AAB, TEX.

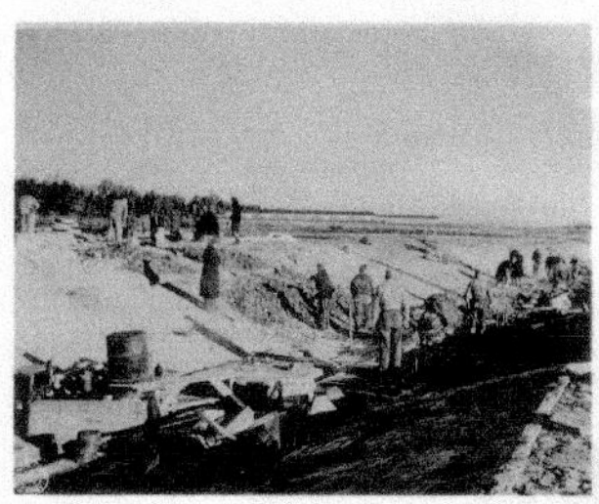

FORT LEONARD WOOD, MO.

WD – ASF – PMGO

PRISONERS OF WAR WORK

POST ENGINEER WORK

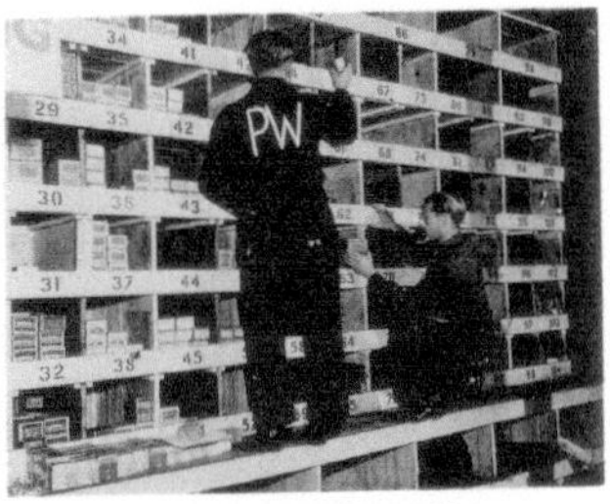

FORT BENJAMIN HARRISON, IND.

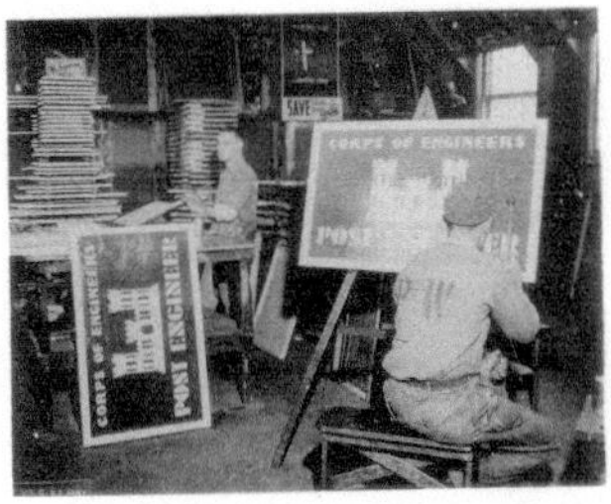

CAMP BRECKINRIDGE, KY.

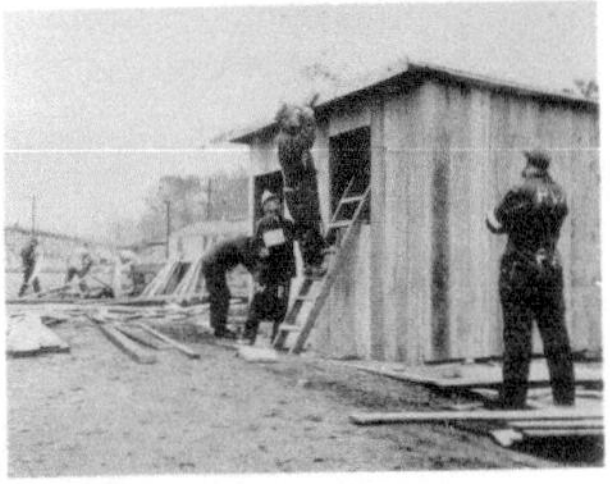

NORFOLK ARMY AIR BASE, VA.

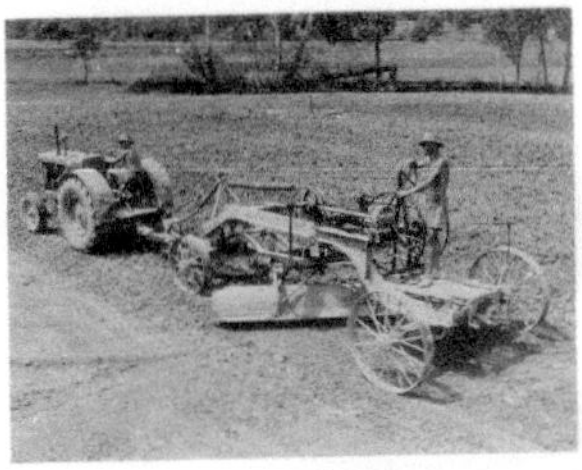

CAMP CLINTON, MISS.

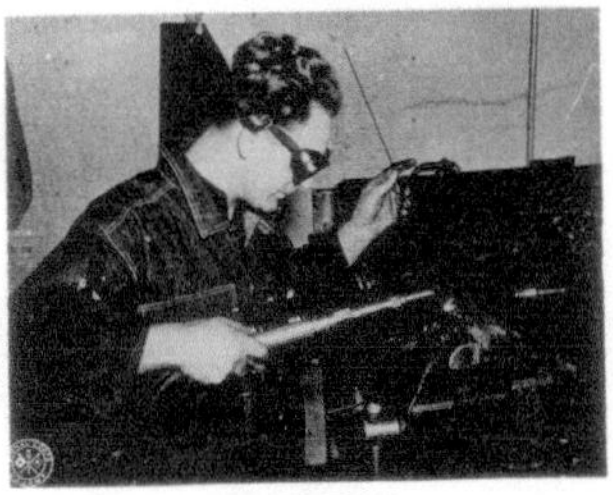

FORT DEVENS, MASS.

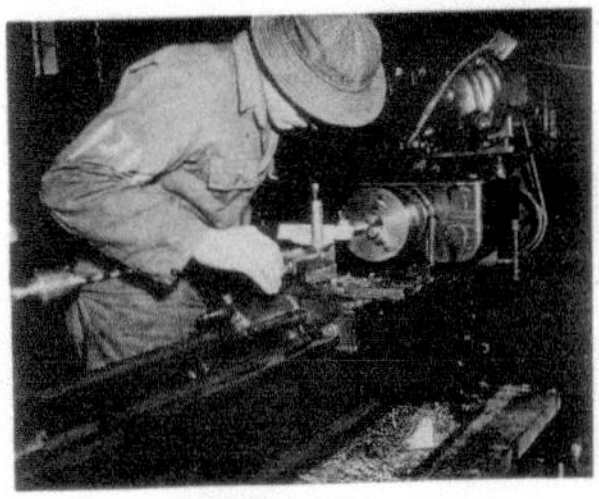

CAMP LEE, VA.

WD - ASF - PMGO

Appendix B

Museums and Websites

Arizona Historical Society Museum, Papago Park, AZ—http://www.arizonahistoricalsociety.org/museums
Billion Graves – www.billiongraves.comCalifornia Military Museum – www.militarymuseum.org, also a brick and mortar location in Sacramento.
Brigham City Museum, 24 N 300 W., Brigham City, UT
Camp Aliceville—www.encyclopediaofalabama.org/face/Article.isp?id-2322.
Camp Hearne Museum – http://camphearne.com/index.htm
Camp Opelika – http://www.eastalabama.org/Exhibits/Exhibits.htm
Camp Ruston – http://www.latech.edu/library/scma/index.php
Camp Van Dorn World War II Museum – www.vandorn.org
Cemetery Records Online—www.interment.net
Door County Maritime Museum, Sturgeon Bay, WI, has display on WWII POWs in the area orchards
Drew County Museum, Monticello, AR, has a display on WWII POWs at Camp Monticello.
Family Search – familysearch.org
Farragut State Park, 13550 E.Hwy 54, Athol, ID, 83801, https://parksandrecreation.idaho.gov/parks/farragut
Find a Grave—www.findagrave.com
Fort Douglas, Salt Lake City, UT – www.fortdouglas.org/about/virtual-tour, also cemetery
Fort George G. Meade Museum—www.ftmeade.army.mil/museum/Museum_POW.html
Fort Leonard Wood Museum—www.visitmo.com/museums-at-fort-leonard- wood.aspx
Gem County Museum, 501 E. First St., Emmett, ID 83617
GenTracer—World War II—www.gentracer.org
Hill Aerospace Museum, Roy, UT
History of Farragut State Park—http://parksandrecreation.idaho.gov/parks/farragut
Library of Congress—catalog.loc.govMarch Field Air Museum, Riverside, CA—www.marchfield.org
Mississippi Armed Forces Museum, Camp Shelby, MS—www.armedforcesmuseum.us/Pages/Newsletter.pdf
Mississippi History Now – http://mshistory.k12.ms.us/index.php?id=233Under
Orem Heritage Museum, Orem, UT
Salina Camp CCC/POW Museum, 700 Main St., Salina, UT, 84654
Traces – www.traces.org
U.K. National Archives—www.nationalarchives.gov.uk
U.S. Dept. of Veterans Affairs National Cemeteries—www.cem.va.gov/cem/cems/listcem.asp
U.S. National Archives—www.archives.gov
U. S. National Park Service—www.nps.gov
Utah State Historical Society Museum, 300 Rio Grande, Salt Lake City, UT
Weber State University, Stewart Library, Special Collections Exhibits, "Prisoners of War in Ogden"—http://library.weber.edu/asc/POW/default.cfm

Bibliography

Adams, Meredith Lentz. "A Miscarriage of Justice?" interview by Jim Kelly. Sunflower Journeys Home 16101A. KTWU. 2003.

_____. *Murder and Martial Justice: Spying and Retribution in World War II America*. Kent, Ohio: Kent State University Press, 2011.

_____. "The Abortive Attempt to Exchange GI and German POWs." (Presentation, TRACES conference, 31 May 2003).

Alberts, Betty. Interview by author. 10 March 2012.

Alexander, Thomas G. "Ogden's Arsenal of Democracy, 1920-1955." *Utah Historical Quarterly* 33 (Summer 1965): 240-245.

_____. "Brief Histories of Three Federal Military Installations in Utah: Kearns Army Air Base." *Utah Historical Quarterly* 34 (Spring 1966): 123-126.

Amdt, Karl John Richard. "German P.O.W. Camp Papers." Microfilm. Washington, D.C.: Library of Congress Photoduplication Service, 1965. Library of Congress. http://lccn.loc.gov/83125121. Accessed September 20, 2012.

Angerilli, Adriano. Interview by author. 14 August 2009.

Army Service Forces. Service Command Operating Personnel and Prisoners, 31 March 1945, NARA RG 389, Entry 261, Box 2563; National Archives at College Park, College Park, MD.

Arrington, Leonard J. and Thomas G. Alexander. "Sentinels on the Desert: The Dugway Proving Ground (1942-1963) and Deseret Chemical Depot (1942-1955)." *Utah Historical Quarterly* 32 (Winter 1964): 32-38.

_____. "Supply Hub of the West: Defense Depot Ogden, 1941-1964." *Utah Historical Quarterly* 32 (Spring 1964): 99-112.

_____. "They Kept 'Em Rolling: The Tooele Army Depot, 1942-1962." *Utah Historical Quarterly* 31 (Winter 1963): 3-14.

_____. "The U.S. Army Overlooks Salt Lake Valley: Fort Douglas, 1862-1965." *Utah Historical Quarterly* 33 (Fall 1965): 326-351.

_____. "World's Largest Military Reserve: Wendover Air Force Base, 1941-63." *Utah Historical Quarterly* 31 (Fall 1963): 324-332.

Arrington, Leonard J., Thomas G. Alexander, and Eugene A. Erb, Jr. "Utah's Biggest Business: Ogden Air Materiel Area at Hill Air Force Base, 1938-1965." *Utah Historical Quarterly* 33 (Winter 1965): 9-16.

Arrington, Leonard J. and Archer L. Durham. "Anchors Aweigh in Utah: The U.S. Naval Supply Depot at Clearfield, 1942 –1962." *Utah Historical Quarterly* 31 (Spring 1963): 109-118.

Bishop, M. Guy. *A History of Sevier County*. Salt Lake City, UT: Utah Historical Society, 1997.

Blanthorn, Ouida. *A History of Tooele County*. Salt Lake City, UT: Utah Historical Society, 1998.

Boudreaux, Henry J, Capt., C.M.P. Report of Investigation of the deaths of Leonello Bini, Vito Clemente,

Adolfo Nitri, Antonino Paleologo, 21 July 1943, NARA RG 389, Entry 461, Box 2562; National Archives at College Park, College Park, MD.

Bryan, B. M., Brigadeer General. Assistant Provost Marshal General, Letter to Army Services Forces regarding transfer of POWs, 26 August 1944, NARA RG 389, Entry 457, Box 1419; National Archives at College Park, College Park, MD.

Bulkat, Ernst. Interview by author. 11 March 2007.

Busco, Ralph A. "A History of the German and Italian Prisoner of War Camps in Utah and Idaho during World War II." (Master's Thesis, Utah State University, 1967).

Busco, Ralph A. and Douglas D. Adler. "German and Italian Prisoners of War in Utah and Idaho." Utah Historical Quarterly 39 (Winter 1971): 55-72.

Busco, Ralph A. "Italian Prisoners of War and Italian Service Unit Camp Newsletters," 1965. Special collections, Merrill-Cazier Library, Utah State University, Logan, Utah.

Bykofsky, Joseph and Harold Larson. *United States Army in World War II: The Technical Services. The Transportation Corps: Operations Overseas.* Center of Military History, United States Army, Washington, D.C., 2003.

Campbell, Eugene E. "The M-Factors in Tooele's History." *Utah Historical Quarterly* 51 (Summer 1983): 272-289.

Carlson, Lewis. "POW Experience: Myth and Reality." (Presentation, TRACES conference, 6 October 2002).

Carter, Andrea Kaye. "Bushnell General Military Hospital and the Community of Brigham City, Utah During World War II." (Master's Thesis, Utah State University, 2008).

Clayton, James L. "An Unhallowed Gathering: The Impact of Defense Spending on Utah's Population Growth, 1940-1964." *Utah Historical Quarterly* 34 (Summer 1966): 218-227.

Conn, Stetson and Byron Fairchild. *The United States Army in World War II, The Western Hemisphere, The Framework of Hemisphere Defense.* Washington, D.C., Office of the Chief of Military History, Department of the Army, 1960.

Conn, Stetson and Rose C Engelman and Byron Fairchild, *The United States Army in World War II, The Western Hemisphere, Guarding the United States and its Outposts.* Washington, D.C., Office of the Chief of Military History, Department of the Army, 1964

Cosentini, George and Norman Gruenzner. United States Numbered Military Post Offices Assignments and Locations 1941-1994. The Military Postal History Society, 1994.

Cowley, Betty. *Stalag Wisconsin: Inside WWII Prisoner-of-war Camps.* Oregon, WI: Badger Books, 2002.

Cunningham, Raymond Kelly. *Prisoners at Fort Douglas: War Prison Barracks Three and the alien enemies, 1917-1920.* Salt Lake City, Utah: Fort Douglas Military Museum, 1983.

Daugherty, Joseph B., Col. Assistant, Office of the Quartermaster General, Letter to Provost Marshal General regarding repatriation of ISU units, dated 9 October 1945, NARA RG 389, Entry 261, Box 2563.

_____. Letter to Provost Marshal General regarding repatriation of ISU units, dated 28 August 1945, NARA RG 389, Entry 261, Box 2563.

"Department of Veterans Affairs National Cemeteries." United States Department of Veterans Affairs, last modified July 13, 2012. http://www.cem.va.gov/cem/cems/listcem.asp.

Ducharme, Joseph O. C., Lt. Col. Director, Enemy PW Information Bureau, Camp Holabird, MD, to Provost Marshal General, regarding cemetery locations, dated 16 February 1953, NARA RG 389, Entry 261, Box 2562.

_____. Regarding cemetery locations, dated 16 February 1953, NARA RG 389, Entry 467, Box 1513.

Dvorak, Petula. "Fort Hunt's Quiet Men Break Silence on WWII." *Washington Post.* 6 October 2007.

Edwards, Earl L., Lt. Col. Asst. Dir., Prisoner of War Division, Letter to Army Services Forces, regarding prisoner segregation, dated 3 March 1944, NARA RG 389, Entry 261, Box 2563.

_____. Letter Regarding Prisoner Transfer, dated 16 October 1943, NARA RG 389, Entry 261, Box 2563.

_____. Letter Regarding Prisoner Transfer, dated 7 January 1943, NARA RG 389, Entry 261, Box 2563.

Embry, Jessie L. "Fighting the Good Fight: The Utah Home Front during World War II." *Utah Historical Quarterly* 63 (Summer 1995): 241-268.

Enemy Prisoner of War Information Bureau. World War II Enemy Prisoners of War Deceased in Theaters of Operations, Fort Holabird, MD, 2 July 1952, NARA RG 389, Entry 466, Box 1.

Erichsen, Heino R. *The Reluctant Warrior: Former German POW Finds Peace in Texas*. Austin, TX: Eakin Press, 2001.

_____. Interview by author. 7 October 2002.

Fairchild, Byron and Jonathan Grossman. *United States Army in World War II: The War Department: The Army and Industrial Manpower*. Center of Military History, Department of the Army, Washington, D.C., 2002.

Farrand, Stephen M. Major, Prisoner of War Operations Division, Letter to Special War Problems Division regarding the death of Karl Schaeffer, dated 28 May 1945, NARA RG 389, Entry 261, Box 2562.

_____. Letter to Special War Problems Division regarding the death of Alfred Malinowski, dated 20 February 1945, NARA RG 389, Entry 261, Box 2562.

"Find a Grave," Find a Grave. http://www.findagrave.com/.

Fischer, H. P., Office of the Commanding General, Ninth Service Command, Fort Douglas, UT, Letter to Army Service Forces regarding new base camps, dated 31 March 1945. NARA RG 389, Entry 457, Box 1419.

Ford, George. "German Guard Held in Medical Ward After Shooting 28 Germans: Probe Opened by Army Into Salina Affair." *The Deseret News*, 9 July 1945.

"Former Prisoner of War Camp," City of Orem, last modified 08 August 2012. http://www.orem.org/index.php?option=com_content&task=view&id=274&Itemid=32

Gansberg, Judith M., *Stalag: U.S.A: The Remarkable Story of German POWs in America*. New York, NY: Thomas Y. Crowell Company, 1977.

Giordana, Beth. Interview by author. August 2001.

Griffith, L. E. Lt. Col., Prisoner of War Operations Division, Letter to Mrs. Ada Errera regarding transfer of body to Italy, dated 30 April 1946, NARA RG 389, Entry 261, Box 2562.

Barbara Schmitter Heisler, "Returning to America: German Prisoners of War and the American Experience." *German Studies Review*, Vol. 31, No. 3 (Oct. 2008), pp. 537-556; Published by: The Johns Hopkins University Press on behalf of the German Studies Association

Heitmann, John A. "Enemies are Human." (Presentation, Dayton Christian-Jewish Dialogue, 10 May 1998).

Holzapfel, Richard Neitzel. *A History of Utah County*. Salt Lake City: Utah State Historical Society, 1999.

Huchel, Frederick M., *A History of Box Elder County*. Salt Lake City, UT: Utah State Historical Society, 1999.

Iannantuoni, Mario. Interview by author. 10 February 2012.

Jones, L. B. C. Lt. Col. Deputy Director, Internal Security Division, Regarding Security, dated 14 October 1943, NARA RG 389, Entry 261, Box 2563.

Keefer, Louis E., *Italian Prisoners of War in America, 1942-1946: Captives or Allies?* New York, NY: Praeger, 1992.

Kirkpatrick, Kathy. "Italian POWs in Utah." (Presentation, TRACES conference, 7 October 2002)

_____ (Presentation, TRACES conference 31 May 2003).

Knappe, Siegfried & Ted Brusaw. *Soldat: Reflections of a German Soldier 1936-1949*. New York, NY: Orion Books, 1992.

Krammer, Arnold. "American Treatment of German Generals." *The Journal of Military History* 54, No. 1 (January 1990): 27-46.

_____. "German Prisoners of War in the United States" *Military Affairs* 40, No. 2 (April 1976): 68-73.

_____. *Nazi Prisoners of War in America*. Lanham, MD: Scarborough House, 1996.

Launius, Roger D. "Crossroads of the West: Aviation Comes to Utah, 1910-40." *Utah Historical Quarterly* 58, Vol. 2 (Spring 1990).

Launius, Roger D. "Home on the Range: The U.S. Air Force Range in Utah, a Unique Military Resource." *Utah Historical Quarterly* 59 (Fall 1991): 332-361.

Launius, Roger D. and Jessie L. Embry. "A Transforming Force: Military Aviation and Utah in World War II." *Utah Historical Quarterly* 63 (Summer 1995): 222-241.

Leighton, Richard M., and Robert W. Coakley. *The United States Army in World War II, The War Department, Global Logistics and Strategy 1940-1943.* Washington, D.C., Office of the Chief of Military History, Department of the Army, 1955.

Leonard, Glen M. *A History of Davis County.* Salt Lake City, UT: Utah State Historical Society, 1999.

Lewis, George G, and John Mewha. *History of Prisoner of War Utilization by the United States Army, 1776-1945.* U.S. Department of the Army, Pamphlet 20-213, Washington, D.C.: Government Printing Office, 1955.

Lucioli, Ezio. Interview by author. 14 August 2009.

Luick-Thrams, Michael. "The Fritz Ritz: German POWs in the American Heartland." (Presentation, TRACES conference, 31 May 2003).

Margotilli, Giuseppe. Interview by author. 14 August 2009.

Martin, Charles E., Col., Director of Personnel, Memorandum to Armed Service Forces, regarding release of ISU, dated 3 October 1945, NARA RG 389, Entry 261, Box 2563.

_____. Memorandum to Armed Service Forces, regarding release of ISU, dated 23 August 1945, NARA RG 389, Entry 261, Box 2563.

_____. Memorandum to Armed Service Forces, regarding release of ISU, dated 20 August 1945, NARA RG 389, Entry 261, Box 2563.

Miller, Orrin P. *History of Tooele County, Vol. II.* Tooele Transcript Bulletin, Tooele, UT, 1990.

Moore, John Hammond. "Italian POWs in America: War is Not Always Hell." Prologue (Fall 1976): 141-151.

_____. *Wacko War: Strange Tales from America 1941-1945.* Raleigh, NC: Pentland Press, 2001.

Nagler, Joerg A. "Enemy Aliens and Internment in World War I: Alvo von Alvensleben in Fort Douglas, Utah, a Case Study." *Utah Historical Quarterly* 58 (Fall 1990): 388-406.

Nash, Gerald D. *The American West Transformed: The Impact of the Second World War.* Bloomington, IN: Indiana University Press, 1985.

National Archive Record Group 389

News of the Week, Utah ASF Depot, Ogden, Utah, 3 September 1943.

Noble, Antonette Chambers. "Utah's Defense Industries and Workers in World War II." *Utah Historical Quarterly* 59 (Fall 1991): 365-380.

_____. "Utah's Rosies: Women in the Utah War Industries During World War II." *Utah Historical Quarterly* 59 (Spring 1991): 123-146.

Orsini, August. Interview by author. 7 October 2011.

Palermo, Raffaele. "ISU Personnel Records." Al Ministero della Difesa, Roma, Italy.

Parri, Dino. *Il Giuramento; Generale a El Alamein, prigioniero in America (1942-1945).* Milano: Mursia, 2009.

"Per il Soldato Francesco Erriquez la guerra è finita!" *Un Mondo di Italiani*, last accessed September 26 2012. http://www.unmondoditaliani.com/per-il-soldato-francesco-erriquez-la-guerra-e-finita.htm.

Peterson, F. Ross. *A History of Cache County.* Salt Lake City, UT: Utah State Historical Society, 1997.

Pisani, Pat and Maria. Interview by author. 12 June 2009.

Poll, Richard D., Utah's History. Provo, UT: Brigham Young University Press, 1978.

Powell, Allan Kent. *Utah Remembers World War II.* Logan, UT: Utah State University Press, 1991.

_____. *Splinters of a Nation; German Prisoners of War in Utah.* Salt Lake City, UT: University of Utah Press, 1989.

_____. "Our Cradles Were in Germany: Utah's German American Community and World War I." *Utah Historical Quarterly* 58 (Fall 1990): 371-388.

Prisoners in Paradise, DVD, directed by Camilla Calamandrei. 2001.

"Prisoners of War in Ogden: 1943-1946." Weber State University Stewart Library, last modified December 23, 2008. http://library.weber.edu/asc/POW/default.cfm.

Pulia, Peter A., Sr. Interview by author. 1 May 2002.

Reiss, Matthias. "Bronzed Bodies behind Barbed Wire: Masculinity and the Treatment of German Prisoners of War in the United States during World War II." *The Journal of Military History* 69, No. 2 (April 2005): 475-504.

Richards, Su. Interview by author. 23 May 2009.

Rogers, John R. Interview by author. 3 September 2007.

Salgado, Rebecca C. "Rebuilding the Network: Interpretation of World War II Prisoner-of-War Camps in the United States." (Master's Thesis, Columbia University, May 2012).

Scott, Ralph. "Violations of International Law in the Treatment of German POWs Following the Cessation of Hostilities". (Presentation, TRACES conference, 1 June 2003).

Smith, Clarence McKittrick. *United States Army in World War II: The Technical Services: The Medical Department: Hospitalization and Evacuation, Zone of Interior*. Center of Military History, United States Army, Washington, D.C., 2003.

Spidle, Jake W. Jr. "Axis Prisoners of War in the United States, 1942-1946: A Bibliographical Essay." Military Affairs 39, No. 2 (April 1975): 61-66.

"State Department-Related Sites: Hotels and Resorts," German American Internee Coalition, last accessed September 20, 2012. http://www.gaic.info/ShowPage.php?section=Internment_Camps.

Thomas, Jennie M. *History of the Prisoner of War Camp Utah ASF Depot*, Ogden, Utah, 1 February 1945.

Thompson, Antonio S., *Men in German Uniform: POWs in America during World War II*. Knoxville, TN: University of Tennessee Press, 2010.

Tissing, Robert Warren Jr. "Utilization of Prisoners of War in the United States During World War II: Texas, A Case Study." (Master's Thesis, Baylor University, 1973).

Todaro, Robert J. Interview by author. 12 June 2006.

Togni, Fernando. Interview by author. 14 August 2009.

Tollefson, A. M., Col., Director, Prisoner of War Operations, Letter to Special Projects Division regarding the death of Giovanni Cincotta, dated 10 January 1946, NARA RG 389, Entry 462, Box 2562.

______. Letter to Special Projects Division regarding the death of Giovanni E. Bondini, dated 8 June 1945, NARA RG 389, Entry 261, Box 2562.

______. Letter to Special Projects Division regarding Salina shooting, dated 28 August 1945, NARA RG 389, Entry 261, Box 2562.

Trezzani, Claudio. Letter from Monticello PW Camp, AR, dated 26 January 1944. Stato Maggiore Esercito, #2256A, Roma.

Ulio, J.A., Major General, the Adjutant General's office, letter to The Commanding Generals, dated 9 April 1943. NARA RG 389, Entry 261, Box 2563.

University of Utah. *Historic Fort Douglas at the University of Utah, a Brief History & Walking Tour*. Salt Lake City, UT: University of Utah, 2000.

Urwiller, Clifford S., Col. Prisoner of War Operations Division, Memorandum for Camp Operations Branch regarding surplus ISU units, dated 18 October 1945, NARA RG 389, Entry 261, Box 2563.

______. Memorandum for Camp Operations Branch regarding surplus ISU units, dated 14 September 1945, NARA RG 389, Entry 261, Box 2563.

U.S. House. Report of Committee on Military Affairs. 78th Congress., 2nd sess., H. Res. 30.

U.S. House. Report of Committee on Military Affairs. 79th Congress., 1st sess., H. Res. 20.

Utah Archives and Records Service, Office of Vital Records and Statistics, Death Certificates

War Department, to Commanding Generals, Regarding movement orders, dated 14 November 1945, NARA RG 389, Entry 261, Box 2563.

______. Regarding movement orders, dated 1 November 1945, NARA RG 389, Entry 261, Box 2563.

______. Regarding movement orders, dated 23 October 1945, NARA RG 389, Entry 261, Box 2563.

______. Regarding movement orders, dated 18 September 1945, NARA RG 389, Entry 261, Box 2563.

Wardlow, Chester. *United States Army in World War II: The Technical Services: The Transportation Corps: Movements, Training, and Supply*. Center of Military History, United States Army, Washington, D.C., 2003.

Weyand, A. M., Col. Commanding, Prisoner of War Camp, Ogden, UT, Letter regarding prisoner segregation, dated 21 January 1944, NARA RG 389, Entry 261, Box 2563.

Wilcox, Walter W. "The Wartime Use of Manpower on Farms." *Journal of Farm Economics* 28, No. 3 (Aug. 1946): 723-741.

Winter, Alexander. "Utah War Industry During World War II: A Human Impact Analysis." *Utah Historical Quarterly* 51 (Winter 1983): 72-93.

Winter, Richard. "Hot Springs, NC. A World War I Internment Camp." *North Carolina Postal Historian* 27, no. 1 (2008).

"WWI German Prisoners of War in Utah," GenTracer, last accessed September 26, 2012. http://www.gentracer.org/WWIGermanPrisonersofWarinUtah.html.

"WWI Internment Camp in Hot Springs, NC: The German Village," Welcome to Madison County, North Carolina, accessed Sept 1, 2012. http://www.visitmadisoncounty.com/who-we-are/town-of-hot-springs/the-german-village-wwi-internment-camp/.

Acknowledgements

Karrie and Jenefer Jackson (data entry)
Kate and John Saffell (website, data entry, photos)
Chris Saffell (researcher and travel companion)
Alessandro de Gaetano (producer, screenwriter of Red Gold)
Barbara Harvey (mother, support, great memory for events in her lifetime, AZ)
Dave Kendziura (historian, Hill AFB, Clearfield, UT) Davis
Gina McNeeley (photographic expert, NARA researcher)
Karen Jensen and Pam Frisbie (my sisters who share the lure of the stories behind the headstones)
Kenneth D. Schlessinger (NARA II, College Park, MD)
Kent Powell (Utah Historical Society, Salt Lake City, UT)
Col. Maurizio Parri (grandson of General Dino Parri, an Italian POW at Camp Monticello, AR)
Michael Luick-Thrams (TRACES founder, IA)
Michael Pomeroy (authority on Camp Monticello, AR)
Rhonda Jackson and Lucia Rogers (researchers, AZ)
Sarah Langsdon (Special Collections, Weber State University, Ogden, UT)
Stefano Palermo (son of Raffaele Palermo, an Italian POW in California and Arizona)
Su Richards (historian, Ft. Douglas Museum, Salt Lake City, UT)

Index